For years, Kim Anderson has been one of my most trusted advisors for my books and research. Her wisdom and insight has made a great difference in my life and the lives of so many – and now it can make a difference in yours. If you feel "stuck" in your personal development, marriage, relationships with friends, or any other area, this book will give you just the tools and encouragement you need to emerge from that rut and fly.

– **SHAUNTI FELDHAHN**, social researcher and best-selling author of *For Women Only* and *Find Rest*

Kim's is a refreshing voice that names what we all know to be true: adults don't always act like adults and, sometimes, we get stuck. *Unstuck* shows women (and this man as well!) how to trade lives of frustration and complacency for purpose and passion, regardless of what the peer pressure might be. Highly recommend!

-**SCOTT SAULS**, pastor of Christ Presbyterian Church in Nashville, Tennessee and author of four books, including *Befriend* and *Irresistible Faith*

For years, Kim has been an exceptional and out of the box coach and counselor, blending brain science and self-development into her own unique approach that has helped shift the lives of many. *Unstuck* shares the very best of her unique perspective and practices. Reading her words feels like there's a hand on your shoulder, comforting you and pushing you forward at the same time. No question in mind, if you're feeling lost, uninspired, overwhelmed or stuck, you're holding hope and help in your hands. Read. This. Book.

-**CHANCE SCOGGINS**, Life & Business Coach, Founder of Life Relaunch

T0098599

Every time I speak on the subject of girls, I talk about how profoundly hard girls are on themselves. And then, I turn to the moms in the room and say, "And you are grown up little girls." This book speaks to the grown-up girl inside of you...who is still profoundly hard on herself, but has found those myths you've believed since somewhere around the age of 13 even more twisted around your heart. I am thrilled to introduce you to Kim Anderson. Her voice is one I trust deeply. It's a voice of compassion, wisdom, warmth, and refreshing truth. This book will help free you from those myths and discover more of who she is cheering you on to be through every page of this book...you!

-SISSY GOFF, Author of *Are My Kids on Track* and
Director of Child & Adolescent Counseling at
Daystar Counseling Ministries, Nashville, TN

Much of our work in caring for kids is supporting moms-reminding them we're on their team and they're doing great, in a world that is heaping expectation, criticism and comparison on them. Kim Anderson is cheering them and helping women dissect the messages they are getting from way too many places. I'm so grateful for Kim and for *Unstuck*.

-DAVID THOMAS, Author of *Intentional Parenting*
and Director of Family Counseling,
Daystar Counseling Ministries, Nashville, TN

Anchored in scripture, *Unstuck* is an encouragement for women to speak truth to one another. Kim not only talks the talk, but walks the walk as well, as she exemplifies the same vulnerability she tells women to embrace and drops the façade of perfection to share her own stories and struggles.

-SARAH NUSE, founder of Tippi Toes Inc, host of
Destined for Greatness podcast and *Shark Tank* alum

For any woman who feels stuck, *Unstuck* covers it all- personal development, relationships with friends, marriage, the whole lot of it. Kim speaks to the hearts of women who have been working at this life thing for a while and lets them know they are not alone. Emerging from the rut is possible.

-LORI ZABKA, Certified Nutrition Coach, Fitness Trainer,
and co-host of the *Coming Un.glued* Podcast

A refusal to watch women punish themselves any longer, *Unstuck* lovingly dispels the myths that keep women stuck.

- CARLA PONCIROLI BABB, LPC-MHSP, Owner,
Cypress Counseling Group, PLLC

You don't have to be a mom or even a Christian to benefit from the timely and practical insight in *Unstuck*. This guide is for any woman who feels stuck and doesn't know how to get past the obstacles in her life.

-NOAH ZAPF, PhD, LPC

Unstuck

unstuck

LETTING GO OF THE MYTHS KEEPING YOU FROM WHO YOU ARE CREATED TO BE

KIM ANDERSON

NEW YORK

LONDON • NASHVILLE • MELBOURNE • VANCOUVER

unstuck

Letting Go of the Myths Keeping You from Who You Are Created to Be

© 2020 Kim Anderson

Published in New York, New York, by Morgan James Publishing. Morgan James is a trademark of Morgan James, LLC. www.MorganJamesPublishing.com

Scripture is from The Holy Bible, English Standard Version. ESV® Text Edition: 2016. Copyright © 2001 by Crossway Bibles, a publishing ministry of Good News Publishers.

The information in this book is based on the research and experience of the author. It is not intended to be medical advice, or to be used as a substitute for consulting with your practioner or physician. The information in this book is to be used for informational and educational purposes only. You must consult your doctor before using any information in this book, changing your lifestyle, or taking up any therapies used or discussed by the author. Kim Anderson, or any persons mentioned in this book, are not responsible for any adverse effects or consequences resulting from the suggestions in the book.

ISBN 9781642794991 paperback
ISBN 9781642795004 eBook
Library of Congress Control Number: 2019902109

Cover Design by:
Ryan Lause
ryanlause91@gmail.com

Interior Design by:
Chris Treccani
www.3dogcreative.net

Interior Graphics by:
Bethany Rogers
www.heyworldcreative.com

Morgan James is a proud partner of Habitat for Humanity Peninsula and Greater Williamsburg. Partners in building since 2006.

Get involved today! Visit
MorganJamesPublishing.com/giving-back

A special thank you to my family, Dave, Keilah, and Luke. Your patience, support, and encouragement mean everything to me. You picked up the slack where I dropped balls in this process, never complaining. You inspire me toward continuous growth and I am grateful for you.

And to the women who have sat with me and shared their stories, thank you for trusting me. I believe your courage will empower others to face their own journeys.

Table of Contents

Introduction

This is the part of the book where I tell you why I am writing. Let me start by saying that I'm *not* writing because the process of writing—sitting for uninterrupted periods of time with only my laptop for company—intrigues me. In fact, sitting alone goes against my extroverted nature. I would rather be doing almost anything than sitting by myself, trying to explain my thoughts through carefully constructed sentences.

Instead, I would much rather be sitting with you at your local coffee shop, getting to know you over a latte. Through conversation, I would learn your story, your struggles, and your hopes and dreams. You might tell me about thoughts and patterns that are keeping you stuck, coming between you and the life you desire. I would want to join with you on your journey, pulling out your inner brilliance and calling attention to all the strengths and resources you already have.

Me and you and a latte—*that's* how I wish this could go down. I would never choose to sit down by myself and write it all out to you. But, over time, I felt the Lord nudging me to share these messages with a wider audience—making the whole coffee shop idea seem a little less feasible.

I felt him telling me it was time: Time to share the hurt I see in my counseling office. Time to write honestly about the grueling pain women face when they believe they are not enough. Time to share how many times I've seen women stay stuck in patterns that don't work for them, rather than risk stepping out into the unknown or uncomfortable. Daily, in my therapy office, I hear women express defeated thoughts: I am not enough. I am alone. No one loves me. I don't matter. I should have done better. I'll never get there. I am too unattractive/overweight/out of shape. I've messed up. I can't be forgiven. I can't bear to be rejected. And in reality, what woman hasn't had one or more of these thoughts?

I am burdened for women who settle for who they *think* others want them to be or who society tells them they should be, rather than leaning into all they are uniquely created for. I am no longer willing to stay silent and watch women punish themselves because they believe they are not good enough. So, I'm done with sitting on the sidelines, watching others give up lives of purpose and passion for lives of frustration and complacency. This hurt and pain and stuck-ness and not-enough-ness is my "why" for writing.

It is time for us, as women, to understand that we are made for lives of true abundance. We must speak truth to each other. We must say it like it is. The Hebrew word *shalom* communicates our intended state. God created us for shalom, for "completeness, wholeness, health, peace, welfare, soundness, tranquility, fullness, rest, and harmony."[1] Let that sink in. If our Creator has so much more for us, then why do we settle for less? Why do we buy the lies that limit our potential?

But, we do. We accept the lies society, media, family, and friends place on us. We accept shame and are ruled by fear. We medicate. We become busy. We stuff our feelings. We pretend not to feel. We blame others for our own situations or wallow in guilt

---

1   James Strong, *The New Strong's Expanded Exhaustive Concordance of the Bible* (Nashville: Thomas Nelson, 2010).

as we blame ourselves. We tell ourselves that it is not fair and other people have it better. We tell ourselves that if we are not perfect, we are not worthy.

I don't have all of the answers for the complexity of modern life, but I do have one: *change starts with you*. You will remain stuck, hopeless, and helpless until you realize you have the power to choose change. Viktor Frankl, psychiatrist and Holocaust survivor, came to a profound realization while in a Nazi concentration camp. In *Man's Search for Meaning*, Frankl writes, "Everything can be taken from a man but one thing: the last of the human freedoms—to choose one's attitude in any given set of circumstances, to choose one's own way."[2] In the camp, where he had no control over his fate, he had hope because he could still choose his attitude, the way he would approach each day.

My friend, no circumstance exists that you cannot choose to see differently. Your thoughts and attitudes are ultimately under your control. Now, I will agree with you that changing entrenched feelings and long-standing perspectives is hard. And certainly you may find yourself in circumstances none of us would choose. But change is possible! It will require commitment and diligence on your part, but do not lose hope.

To be clear, no one else can do the work for you. I will cheer you on and give you lots to think about, but, ultimately, we all have to face our own stories, struggles, and fears. I know because I have had to do my own work, too. I have had to be vulnerable, honest, and real with myself and others in the name of change. But I continue to push past the hurdles because I know that, as scary as change can be, it is so much better on the other side. We will always have struggles, but the work is worth it. Choose the work.

---

2   Viktor Frankl, *Man's Search for Meaning* (Boston: Beacon Press, 2016).

You may even find it empowering to finally face fears, troubling circumstances, and heavy emotions head-on. This means you stop running. You come out of the shadows and choose to be brave instead. You dare to hold your problems up to a full-length mirror and face the parts that must change. After all, we cannot be a light to those around us when we cloak our struggles in darkness and refuse to see ourselves clearly.

In this book, I share sixteen myths that keep many women stuck and prevent us from living our lives with purpose and passion. You might identify with all of them, some of them, or none of them. My hope is that you can sit in a quiet space and dig deep. Take a long look at your excuses, your battles, and your defeated thought patterns. Face your obstacles and ask yourself which factors are keeping you stuck. Each chapter has questions at the end, with space to journal. Don't miss the opportunity to self-reflect and examine what might be getting in the way of freedom. You deserve it.

I have had wonderful, amazing teachers, read life-impacting books, and experienced the power of change as I have witnessed clients step out and embrace fear. While I have attempted to give credit to every person who I have learned from, I know I will fall short. Some of the information I share is from those much wiser than me, and some is just common knowledge from the helping industry. I am grateful to every person who has shared in my journey of growth.

Friends, don't let your challenges become your identity. And don't let the story of your past define you either. Other chapters of your life are waiting to be written; bold plot twists and happy endings are still possible. Stop dreaming and start doing. You are created for more, and we need *you*.

If I'm Perfect, My Life Will Be Perfect Too

Perfectionism is the voice of the oppressor, the enemy of the people. It will keep you cramped and insane your whole life.
–ANNE LAMOTT

Our teenage daughter Keilah (Pronounced Kyla. I know. It's tricky.) is extremely organized. She came out of the womb color coding her closet, sorting her socks, labeling her stuffed animals, and stacking the books on her shelf just right. She can spend hours in her room, happily putting everything where it belongs.

When she was in lower elementary school, she would cry once school was out for the summer because she missed the structure and stimulation school provided. As a clueless new mom, exasperated with trying to keep her in a routine, I had no idea what to do. Finally, I had an idea. The summer after kindergarten, in an attempt to provide structure at home—where there wasn't much—I took a piece of poster board and created a "summer schedule," similar to the schedule she had on her wall in school. I hung it on the wall

1

of our kitchen and figured she could reference it when she needed. This schedule broke down our day by the half hour, meaning every minute of the day was spoken for. Every single minute. She absolutely loved it. It made her happy to know she had a plan for the day—although it made me look completely neurotic to my friends. I definitely got some weird looks.

Keilah has always had a plan and has executed it with extreme perfection her whole life. She sets the bar high and excels in anything she puts her mind to. The problem for Keilah is that she was born to a mom who is *anything* but organized. I am the chaos to her calm. I am the tornado to her yellow brick road. Not only do I get in the way of her picture of perfection, I am often its ruin. I am a hot-mess mom on wheels.

Perfectionism has worked for Keilah. It sets her up for success. It keeps her on top of life and living at her best. But, Keilah, like all of us, must be mindful to not take perfectionism too far. She must work to ensure it is not an idol. She has to choose not to anchor her self-worth to a flawless performance. Friends, we must guard our hearts against perfectionism.

Just to be clear, I am *not* talking about the kind of perfectionism that simply motivates us to be our best selves. Rather, I am talking about toxic perfectionism, the kind that sabotages our peace and hijacks our every thought, the kind that keeps us stuck and makes us feel inadequate. Toxic perfectionism comes from an overwhelming desire for acceptance and a paralyzing fear of rejection. It causes us to evaluate our self-worth through a pass-fail lens. If we're not careful, even love can feel conditional, leaving us stressed out over our perfect execution of life and relationships. Perfectionism can lead us to control our interpersonal relationships, overextending ourselves to the point of exhaustion. It can also leave us with the feeling that we need to look as if we have it all together in order to feel accepted. Our house must be perfect, our marriage must be perfect, the kids must perform, and the laundry must be done (and put away). This type of performance keeps our relationships on the surface, and our connections with others limited.

Brené Brown, author, social worker, and shame researcher, writes, "Perfectionism is not the same thing as striving to be your best. Perfectionism is the belief that if we live perfect, look perfect, and act perfect, we can minimize or avoid the pain of blame, judgement, and shame. It's a shield. It's a twenty-ton shield that we lug around thinking it will protect us when, in fact, it's the thing that's really preventing us from flight."[3] Wow. Perfectionism is a weight. It burdens us and slows us down. It promises safety from pain and shame, but it actually generates its own pain as it makes us feel small and inadequate.

And, here's the problem: the perfectionist cannot enjoy rest. Once a goal is attained, the bar is raised. The goal must not have been lofty enough if we were actually able to reach it; we must do better and do more, so we engage in silent competition with ourselves and others. Sadly, all this striving and struggling keeps us from experiencing joy, fulfillment, or pride. We can't experience the peace and satisfaction of a job well done or celebrate our successes if the target is always moving. If our efforts are never quite good enough, we won't feel good at all. Perfectionism is the enemy of contentment and the author of anxiety.

> Perfectionism is the enemy of contentment and the author of anxiety.

---

3   Brené Brown, *The Gifts of Imperfection: Let Go of Who You Think You're Supposed to Be and Embrace Who You Are* (Center City, MN: Hazelden, 2010).

It can even lead to depression if we listen to its lies for long enough. At its extreme, perfectionism is never satisfied. Nothing will ever be good enough. And many of us have some degree of this not-good-enough complex, whether we were born this way or had life experiences that shaped us toward this thinking. We torment ourselves, thinking we are unacceptable to the people around us. Disappointment eventually sets in as we fear we will never, ever get to a level of attainment and status that others will call success. Basically, we settle for less.

The Modern Woman

Let's face it. It is difficult being a woman today. We are compared to impossible standards of perfection and bombarded by airbrushed images on magazines and billboards. Models are anorexic, and most pictures on social media have filters, yet we accept these benchmarks as gospel truth. From all available evidence, women never age or gain weight or have a bad hair day. Amidst the onslaught of perfect abs and fabulous blowouts, how can we not feel the pull of perfection?

And if you're a mom, you get it from all sides. Not only should you look pre-baby fit and achieve exceptional career success, but you must also be the perfect parent. Mom shame is at an all-time high. You might relate to this quote I found on Facebook:

> How to parent in 2018: Make sure your children's academic, emotional, psychological, mental, spiritual, physical, nutritional, and social needs are met while being careful not to overstimulate, under-stimulate, improperly medicate, helicopter, or neglect them in a screen-free, processed food-free, GMO-free, negative

energy-free, plastic-free, body positive, socially conscious, egalitarian but also authoritative, nurturing but fostering of independence, gentle but not overly permissive, pesticide-free, two-story, multi-lingual home, preferably in a cul-de-sac with a backyard and 1.5 siblings spaced at least two years apart for proper development, and also don't forget the coconut oil.

How to parent in literally every other generation before: *Feed them sometimes.*

We can't win. It is not enough to care for our kids and provide a safe, loving home. No, we are expected to read up and be prepared for anything and everything that could possibly go wrong. We are expected to foster optimal brain development, enroll them in competitive sports, and teach them a second language. And if we mess up and raise *only* a happy, healthy kid, well, we are shamed by other moms and often by ourselves. Where did we get these ridiculous standards? And what is the cost of using these standards as noble goals?

Ladies, it's time to back up and ask a few questions. We can't accept the perfect-mom messages society is sending. If you spend even part of your day feeling less than and pressuring yourself to reach some impossible standard, you owe it to yourself to consider the role perfectionism may be playing in your life. Let's consider the story of a former client who learned to put perfectionism in its place. Her story is applicable to all because it shows the danger of anchoring self-worth to performance and unrealistic standards.

Jennifer's Story: The Hamster Wheel of Perfection

Jennifer is a thirty-year-old single female who struggled with anxiety. She came to me feeling uneasy about several things in her life, including work, but her stress was particularly intense any time her parents came to visit.

She reported growing up in a house where she could never be "good enough." Her parents were clear about their disappointment when she obtained anything less than an "A" on a report card. They told her lower grades were unacceptable and that she needed to try harder, despite her rigorous coursework and disciplined study habits. To meet their expectations, she got less than six hours of sleep a night; it was all she could manage while keeping up with her classes and balancing extracurricular activities. She was accepted into a competitive college, but her parents told her they had held higher hopes for her.

Her mother critiqued her appearance much of her childhood. She never seemed to be wearing the right thing, and her weight was a constant topic of discussion. Her mom would comment disapprovingly when what she was wearing was not flattering of her "large frame." Deep into our work, she realized that her previous challenges with bulimia might have come from the desire to control her weight and please her parents. Jennifer met disapproval from her parents at every turn and could never get it right.

Jennifer and I discussed her approach to life and her ongoing desire to achieve perfection in all areas. When she began working with me, she was certain that the pressure she put on herself was a good thing. After all, it had been modeled for her, and it led to what would be deemed by any outsider as a "successful life." She was a respected businesswoman who had accumulated accolades and awards over the years. Because she had done everything the "right" way, she believed wholeheartedly that everything "should" feel so much better for her.

Eventually, Jennifer was able to connect the dots in her own story and saw how perfectionism was getting in the way of living life freely. It was a false self, a mask she hid behind because she felt less-than. Perfectionism seemed to offer her assurance, a way to make sure she was acceptable. Over time, however, she became stuck in a prison of performance, one she was constructing for herself.

She slowly realized that she was not only putting her expectations of perfectionism on herself but also on those around her. Friends had let her know they found her too critical. While she had initially dismissed these comments as jealousy, digs at her success, she was eventually able to accept their feedback. She was even able to track how her critical voice was showing up in her dating relationships as well.

How difficult it is to find peace with self or others when we are stuck in the role of the exacting critic! It's hard to appreciate what you have in the moment when you are calculating what needs to be changed. This mind-set can even lead to resentment when others don't meet your standards or when others don't seem to be working as hard as you are to improve things.

Slowly, Jennifer moved toward a healthy balance of self-compassion and self-improvement. She had to continually fight the deep-seated tendency to treat herself like the enemy any time she made a mistake. Eventually, however, she was able to move toward healthier relationships as she learned to offer love, acceptance, and grace to both herself and others. Jennifer had to make the daily choice to be mindful about her thoughts. She had to choose to detach her value from her performance and accept mistakes as part of the human experience.

Truth 1: Perfectionism Kills Confidence

Perfectionism is the killer of our confidence. To be confident, we must take action and embrace risk, yet perfectionism tells us to play it safe and stick to what we know we're good at. It keeps us stuck in the same safe ruts and on the hamster wheel. Those who are truly confident know how to learn from their mistakes. They aren't scared to slip up because they know every failure has a lesson, and these lessons eventually add up to mastery, calm assurance, and proficiency. Contrast this process to walking the tightrope of perfectionism. On the tightrope, you dare not fall; mistakes are seen as certain death, not opportunities for growth and life.

In *The Confidence Code for Girls*, authors Katty Kay and Claire Shipman write, "While confidence is partly influenced by genetics, it is not a fixed psychological state. You won't discover it by thinking positive thoughts or telling yourself (or your children) that you are perfect as you are. You won't find it either by simply squaring your shoulders and faking it. But it does require a choice: less worrying about people-pleasing and perfection and more action, risk taking, and fast failure."[4] More action! More risk-taking! Maybe even more fun because, let's be real, perfectionism is no fun. It's an obstacle, a true hinderance to the life of peace and serenity we are after.

To overcome toxic perfectionism and take back our freedom, we must have the courage to be authentic. We must go off script and learn to be okay with improvisation. Can we plan? Sure. But, we must not lose our joy when our plan falls through or our results are less than we hoped. We must love ourselves and grow in confidence that God has a plan for our unique gifts and talents.

---

4   Katty Kay and Claire Shipman, *The Confidence Code for Girls: Taking Risks, Messing Up, and Becoming Your Amazingly Imperfect, Totally Powerful Self* (New York: HarperCollins, 2018).

To feel that kind of confidence, we must let go of impossible, perfectionistic standards and choose to throw away the measuring rod. Instead, we choose to love ourselves for who we are and stand tall right where we are, right in the middle of growing and becoming. Confidence is a choice, and you can choose it now. Don't tell yourself that you will be confident once you have polished every rough edge and achieved your impossible goals. Be a confident, courageous woman *now* and watch how others react as you drop the façade of perfection.

Truth 2: Perfectionism Can Show up in Many Different Areas

So far I've focused on perfectionism in external performance or appearance, but perfectionism can show up in other ways as well. For example, some of us overmanage the relationships in our lives so that we will be accepted. That's me. I am a relationship perfectionist.

I have created my own nonclinical diagnosis called RMD: Relationship Management Disorder. (You won't find this diagnosis in the *DSM*-5, by the way.) Perfectionism doesn't show up for me in needing *thing*s to be "just right" or in organization, but perfectionism shows up for me in relationships. I can barely handle it if I have a conflict with someone. Actually, it's not the conflict that bothers me; it's not *resolving* the conflict that bothers me. If I say something that was misinterpreted or put my foot in my mouth, which I do very often, I will ruminate on my misstep for days. Guess what I have had to learn and accept? It is okay to disappoint people. And, it is okay to be disappointed. I'm not perfect and neither are the loved ones I am in relationship with.

Really. It's okay not to be the perfect friend, wife, daughter, PTA member, colleague . . . You get the point.

This sounds obvious, but it took me a long time to let myself off the hook. Avoiding people's disappointment was something I carried around like a two-hundred-pound weight for most of my life, dragging it with me everywhere I went. I felt I could stay safe only if I kept all my people happy at all times. People-pleasing was my refuge, and I couldn't be okay unless everyone around me was okay.

I am not sure where this compulsion began, perhaps it's just the way I am wired. Some personality types have this tendency more than others. Regardless, it was unhealthy in me as I took the tendency to want to help and please to the extreme. I was all too willing to sacrifice my own well-being to make somebody else happy, and this habit took its toll. I matured significantly when I did my own work in therapy and learned I was giving everybody else oxygen but not keeping any for myself.

Little by little, I began taking care of me. I began speaking the truth, even if I knew it would cause disappointment. I began saying no to things that weren't for me, even if it would make someone upset. I learned it wasn't my job to make or keep others happy. Rather, it is my job to love God and to love others. And, sometimes, loving others means letting them experience their own feelings and allowing them to choose how they will experience disappointment. That friend that expects you to meet all of her needs, just might have to be let down. It's okay. That relative that expects you to show up at every family gathering might be upset. That's okay too. Do yourself a favor and let go of their expectations.

Somehow, we've bought the lie that loving someone means doing everything he or she wants, even if it doesn't work for us, even if it compromises who we are. That isn't love. That's *bondage*. We are created to love freely, not under compulsion. After all, if we are gritting our teeth while doing the favor or giving in to the other, is it really love, or is it obligation? Serving others out of guilt or fear of disappointing them is not true service. The next time you feel compelled to say yes, consider your why: why are you helping, sacrificing, or rearranging your plan? Are you compelled by joy and love, or are you driven by panic over the other's reaction if you say no?

Letting go of relationship perfectionism wasn't easy. It took practice, but it was worth it. I encourage you to do the same. Give yourself permission to examine your motives and give yourself permission to disappoint people. When you are honest with yourself and consider your own needs and emotional health as part of the equation, you will actually have more love to give. You will be free to love without resentment, which is the best kind of love.

Have I hammered it in enough? Perfectionism may be keeping you from the freedom and joy you were created for. When we attach our self-worth to performance, status, success, appearance, friend groups, what people think of us, or social media "likes," we will never rest. We are empty because we don't understand our inherent worth as a child of God. The truth is, we are worthy just because God created us and says we are—not because we perform perfectly.

Do you remember the Bible story of God selecting David to rule his people? Samuel, the chief priest, felt certain that God would select the oldest, most physically imposing of Jesse's sons to anoint as king, but God selected the youngest, David: "The Lord said to Samuel . . . The Lord does not look at the things people look at. People look at the outward appearance, but the Lord looks at the heart" (1 Sam. 16:7). When we anchor our self-worth to Christ, we are whole. We know that we are enough, regardless of our appearance, circumstances, or performance. We can rest. We can stop proving. We can stop the game. We can be free.

Do This Instead: Work Towards Unconditional Love

1. Give Mercy in the Mirror

Now that we've diagnosed the problem of toxic perfectionism, how do we tackle it? First, we need to be mindful of our mindset. What is our self-talk? What are the stories we are telling ourselves? Are they true, or are they lies? Are we constantly searching for evidence that we have fallen short and are worthless? If we continue to see life through the lens of not-enough and keep-trying, then even our successes will look like failures.

Researchers call this "confirmation bias," meaning we look for and interpret information that will confirm what we already think is true. Thus, us perfectionists may struggle to see the good in what we accomplish. We may unintentionally look for the flaws, which will confirm our worst fears: I am not enough; I could do better. Without conscious effort to stop these biased thoughts, we will continue to disregard truth and stick to our flawed perspective. So, overcoming this habit of perfectionism, which you've spent years acquiring, may take some effort.

To that end, you must learn to give yourself mercy. *Mercy* is "compassion or forgiveness shown toward someone whom it is within one's power to punish or harm."[5] And, friends, it is definitely within our power to harm our own sense of worth.

> People who tend to be perfectionistic may offer mercy to others who make mistakes but refuse to offer it to themselves.

Every time you hold yourself to an unrealistic standard or berate yourself with negative self-talk, you are punishing yourself. Yet mistakes are part of the human condition. Accept it. We *all* make mistakes. People who

---

5   *Oxford Dictionary*, https://en.oxforddictionaries.com/definition/mercy.

tend to be perfectionistic may offer mercy to others who make mistakes but refuse to offer it to themselves. They can't handle letting themselves down. How about agreeing that we all get to be human? *You* get to be a human. *You* get to mess up. And so do I. We need to see our mistakes and learn from them. Focus on what you are becoming. Focus on where the journey is going, not what you wish you could change about your past.

2. Fail Forward

We also need to look at failure as a gift. Failure teaches us lessons we would otherwise miss. Thomas Edison is famous because he learned from his failures and refused to play it safe. While struggling to invent and innovate, he commented, "I have not failed. I've just found 10,000 ways that won't work."

Failure is only a threat if we give it power. It's all about perspective. What if, instead of catastrophizing, we tell ourselves, "A loss is just a loss, and mistakes are just mistakes. They don't deserve my time or energy, and they certainly don't deserve my power." Try it. Next time you feel perfectionism coming over you, speak that sentence out loud. It is truth. Our success or failure does not define who we are. It is just part of our story. Failure is what makes us likeable, approachable, and authentic. In contrast, others are actually turned off by plastic people who hide all their flaws. When we show humility and vulnerability, we actually draw people toward us. We invite greater intimacy without our fake mask of perfection.

> Our success or failure does not define who we are.

> We invite greater intimacy without our fake mask of perfection.

Failure just gives us the opportunity to try again, from a new angle.

3. Embrace Freedom

We are created to be free: "It is for freedom that Christ has set us free. Stand firm, then, and do not let yourselves be burdened again by a yoke of slavery" (Gal. 5:1). Do you get it? We are completely free because of God's sweet grace. We are free to live. We are free to love ourselves, and we are free to love others. Why take up the burden of perfectionism when the gift of freedom and rest is ours? Claim it today. God loves us just the way we are, and until we love ourselves, we can't love others well.

Ladies, we are not meant to beat ourselves up. Peace comes when we stop judging our weight, our hair, or our skin. Peace is ours when we let go of unrealistic expectations. We must shift our mind-set so that we can be free to love ourselves, love others, and just be. This can be difficult to do, especially for those of us who have been in this pattern for a while. If you identify with these thoughts, I encourage you to work with someone who can walk through this journey with you, so you can step into freedom.

I beg you. Take risks. Mess up. Embarrass yourself. Love yourself. Surround yourself with people who will embrace your imperfections and love you for you, not for your performance. Approach the world with confidence, even if you aren't quite feeling it yet. When you act as if you are confident, others will respond positively, which then makes you confident.

Reflection Questions:

1.	In what ways do you put unrealistic pressure on yourself to be perfect?

2. What messages did you receive growing up that influenced your belief that performance determines your value and worth? How do these messages impact you now?

3. How do your expectations of perfection negatively impact those around you (spouse, children, family, friends, coworkers)? How can you let go of rigid, unrealistic standards?

New Insight:

_____

_____

_____

_____

_____

_____

_____

_____

_____

_____

_____

_____

Other People's Lives
Are So Much Better

A candle loses nothing by lighting another candle.
-JAMES KELLER

For several years on social media, I watched a group of friends document their time together. They would go on adventurous trips (and post their pictures). They would celebrate each other's birthdays (and post their pictures). They would share inside jokes together, demonstrating their tight bonds (and post those moments, too). This was a group of women I longed to be a part of. I really liked them. I felt connected to them. I couldn't, however, figure out a way to get "in"; I didn't know how to crack the code. Yet every time I opened social media, there they were. Together. Having more fun than I was—*or at least that was the lie I told myself.*

Can you relate? You likely know what I am talking about. Have you ever felt the sting of jealousy wash over you as you check your social media accounts? Have you ever started the day with joy, only to become discontent when you log on to see what's new? You see the organic meal she made from scratch for her family.

(She just happened to have everything she needed growing in her garden out back!) You see the Pinterest-worthy birthday party, the one for her one-year-old, who won't even remember.

And how about her *amazing* husband? She gushes in post after post about how he spoils her so. You know, sending flowers "just because." You want to feel happy for her, but the dissatisfaction you feel in your marriage makes her status update too much to bear. And then you see the gifted-beautiful-smart-talented-musical-athletic child who made the honor roll *again*—and the mother who "couldn't help but share." It's not that you wish her or her child ill, but you wonder how much longer your child will just barely squeak by. The homework battle never seems to end, and it is grueling, day after blessed day.

> No one's life is as flawless as it looks online.

Everywhere we turn, we are bombarded with people's "perfect" lives. (Spoiler alert: no one's life is as flawless as it looks online.) Before social media, we took in others' lives in small doses and didn't have access to the personal details of hundreds of acquaintances. We would likely never see the pictures from our college roommate's recent vacation to Paris; we would never hear details about our second cousin's gifted child. But now we see it all—every stinking detail. It is in our face, and the only way to get away from it is to unplug from social media altogether.

Callie's Story: The Best Game is the Worst Trap

Callie was a thirty-five-year-old, married mother of three. Struggles with anxiety led her to therapy, and she described feeling consumed with emotions. In an attempt to numb the pain her emotions and anxiety caused, she would eat, shop, or spend countless hours absorbed in social media.

During therapy, Callie bemoaned that her neighbors' kids were outperforming her kids in sports, and her best friend's kids were outperforming her kids in academics. She noted that her neighbor bought the "best" house in the neighborhood, while she regretted the purchase of her own home as, in hindsight, she saw so many things wrong with it. Callie also mentioned posting the same pictures on social media that her friend posted from a shared event; she was crushed when her friend's post received twice as many "likes."

Even though Callie and her husband wisely created a budget for vacations, she was jealous that they would stay home during an upcoming school break while her friends traveled to the beach. Her husband, in an attempt to please her, acquiesced and made plans to go to the beach. When they got there, she was disappointed that their beach house was not as nice as her friend's.

Sadly, Callie's story is similar to many others I hear in my counseling office. She has spent her life in comparison, believing the lie that everyone else has a better, easier, more desirable life. She is eaten up with envy for the perfect spouse, the perfect kids, the perfect house, the perfect lifestyle, and the perfect . . . well, everything.

Unfortunately, her feelings of "less-than" tainted her interactions with others, and her bitter countenance pushed people away. No one wanted to enter her competition, and her anxiety made it difficult to connect in authentic ways. She couldn't figure out why others didn't include her.

Callie was stuck, and instead of leaning into the discomfort of her emotions, asking what they were telling her, she attempted to numb them. But it doesn't work. Numbing emotions only stuffs them deeper and creates new problems. No wonder she was feeling more and more anxious. Every time she compared herself, her husband, her kids, or her circumstances to someone else's, she was left feeling miserable and even more distressed, which led to more isolation. It was a lose-lose cycle.

Truth 1: Your Heart Closes When You Compare

We women are, arguably, the most prone to comparison. Too often, instead of cheering each other on and affirming the choices of another, we judge. We judge others' appearance, their personal decisions, and their approach to motherhood. Just think of all the hotly contested parenting debates: stay-at-home mom vs. working mom; decided not to have kids vs. six kids and counting; breast feeding vs. formula; organic food vs. conventional; Pampers vs. cloth diapers; day care vs. nanny. Too often, we put down the other camp just to feel better about our own decisions. But sizing up and cutting down others doesn't make us feel better for long. It's only a matter of time until we move on to our next insecurity, wondering how we measure up and how "she" does it "all."

Here's the thing we must remember. When we approach life from a place of not-enough, we become jealous and discontent, and we are robbed of joy. We are robbed of peace, and we are robbed of power. When we compare ourselves to others, it is as if we are walking around with a measuring stick, trying to calculate how we compare. Our mood can go up or down, based on the calculations we make.

> When we compare, we are not comparing our circumstances to the reality of another's life; we are only comparing our life to the *image* of another's life—the one they polish, shine, and post.

The problem is, the measuring stick is faulty. It can't measure accurately because the numbers are in the wrong place.

Why do you think that is? It's because each stick is relative to *our own story*, our unique, one-of-a-kind story. No one can measure or compare her life to the life you have lived. Also, the truth is, things are *never* the way they look. We never know the private battle someone is facing. When we compare, we are not comparing our circumstances to the reality of another's life; we are only comparing our life to the *image* of another's life—the one they polish, shine, and post. Or we may be comparing our life to the image we create in our minds about what their lives *must be like*. And who wouldn't feel depressed when up against a fairy-tale narrative that isn't even true?

We tell ourselves that everyone else has a better life. We are the one missing out; we are the one defective person in our zip code. When we get so caught up in other people's lives, we eventually forget to appreciate what we do have. Brené Brown cautions against this dangerous form of comparison in her book *Rising Strong*:

> The fear of missing out (FOMO) is what happens when scarcity slams into shame. FOMO lures us out of our integrity with whispers about what we could or should be doing. FOMO's favorite weapon is comparison. It kills gratitude and replaces it with "not enough." We answer FOMO's call when we say YES but we really mean NO. We abandon our path and our boundaries and those precious adventures that hold meaning for us so we can prove we aren't missing out. But we are. We are missing out on our own lives. Every time we say YES because we are afraid of missing out, we say NO to something. That something might be

a big dream or a short nap. We need both. Courage
to stay our course and gratitude for our path will
keep us grounded and guide us home.[6]

When we live in the world of comparison, nothing is ever
enough. Fixated on the journey of another, we lose our way on
the path meant for us. We lose the opportunity to celebrate the
blessings we have and to experience the gratitude that comes when
we learn to trust we are right where we are supposed to be.

Truth 2: You Are a DIVINE Masterpiece

During his seventh-grade year, our son, Luke, brought home
artwork he had been working on in his art class. Art was a new
talent for him, one he had not previously realized he possessed. He
was so proud of his work and loved sharing his new creations with
us. One day, I mentioned hanging his art up in the house so that it
could be on display.

He said, "That would be great, but my favorite picture is still
on display at school."

"Great!" I said. "I would love to go up and see it, and I'll take
a picture of you in front of it, to remember how it was displayed."

Luke suddenly got quiet. The big smile on his face when we
were discussing his artwork quickly turned to a look of concern.
I wasn't sure what was going on inside that teenage brain, so I
leaned in.

"What are you thinking, buddy?" I asked.

He said, "That's fine. I'll just bring it home."

---

6   Brené Brown, *Rising Strong: How the Ability to Reset Transforms the Way We
     Live, Love, Parent, and Read* (New York: Random House, 2017).

Confused, I leaned in more. "Are you saying you don't want me to come and see your art on display?"

"Well . . . " he paused. "Other good pictures are up at the school, and they might make mine not look as good," he said with a slight laugh.

I could see it clearly now. He thought I was going to compare his work to the other pieces on display and suddenly see the faults. "Oh, Luke. Are you saying you think I would value your artwork less by seeing the other beautiful pieces of art?"

He laughingly nodded his head. He realized it was a silly notion, yet those feelings of inadequacy still came up for him.

"Luke, do you understand that your artwork is special to me because it is *yours*? It represents you and your heart. It is your own *unique* masterpiece. I would never compare your artwork to anyone else's, any more than I would compare you to anyone else. You are mine, and I cherish you for who you are."

His smile came back. He knew we loved his art because it was *his*, yet deep inside, he still compared himself to the others and thought we might compare him, too.

Don't we get caught in the same dilemma? God created each of us as a masterpiece, but the apostle Paul knew we would forget, so he wrote a reminder to the first-century church: "For we are his workmanship, created in Christ Jesus for good works, which God prepared beforehand, that we should walk in them" (Eph. 2:10).

We are his unique piece of art, created in his image. While

> While we may still look to the right and to the left, examining where we fall short and sizing up the competition, God sees us as beautiful and complete.

we may still look to the right and to the left, examining where we fall short and sizing up the competition, God sees us as beautiful and complete.

Friends, own it. You are a masterpiece. You are his work of art. Picture him saying, "Do you understand that you are special to me because I created you?" He cherishes you exactly the way you are—scars, blemishes, and bruises included. Yes, you are loved exactly how you are.

Do This Instead: Work Towards Contentment

1. Practice Self-Compassion

Instead of falling into the trap of comparison, I encourage you to practice self-compassion. How do I do that, you may be asking yourself? Well I admit it's a practice, like going to the gym or yoga, or eating healthier. Self-compassionate people talk to themselves the way they would talk to someone they love. They treat themselves like they would treat their best friend. They expect of themselves what they would expect of a stranger. They give the same grace to themselves as they would to someone who has wronged them.

Self-compassionate people don't carry measuring sticks; instead, they give *and* receive grace, which is *unmerited* favor. And self-compassionate people can experience true joy because they are *free* from impossible expectations. Very often, women who struggle with self-compassion punish themselves any time they deviate from the primrose path of sunshine and rainbows.

Yet, author Kristin Neff explains that to be content, women must accept a full range of experience and emotion: "Happiness stems from loving ourselves and our lives exactly as they are, knowing that joy and pain, strength and weakness, glory and failure are all essential to the full human experience."[7] What about that? Happiness comes from being okay with pain and failure, too. It comes when you let go of comparing your season and your circumstance to that of another. We are all meant to live in the full range of human experience. Sometimes we are up; sometimes we are down. But pain or failure doesn't mean we have less or are less.

Self-compassion is likely a muscle you'll need to exercise to strengthen. Self-pity seems to come naturally, so it might take conscious effort to lean toward compassion instead. A particularly helpful way to practice self-compassion is through mindfulness, which is the art of bringing our attention to the particular emotions we are feeling at the moment. We notice our thoughts, feelings, bodily sensations—*without judgment.* We notice what are we feeling in our body and thinking in our mind, and then we *let it go.* When we are mindful, we have power over our emotions and fears because we know we get to be in charge of what we are telling ourselves. We can notice the emotion, thank the emotion, and then make a choice about how to steward it. I've included a "Mindfulness Exercise" in the appendix to help you adopt this practice today, if you wish.

Ladies, we are not just learning self-compassion for our own sake. This is about our children as well. Your children are watching you, and they are likely going to take on the same thoughts and emotions you exude. Did you know that children absorb the emotions of the adults around them? If we can't regulate our fears and destructive thoughts, how will they learn? When they watch us throw shade on our appearance or achievement—never satisfied,

---

7   Kristin Neff, *Self-Compassion: The Proven Power of Being Kind to Yourself* (New York: HarperCollins, 2011).

never secure—how will they believe us when we tell them they are enough?

So, start with building personal self-awareness. Be mindful about how you are experiencing your circumstances and the related messages your attitude and expressions are sending to your kids. Do they see self-compassion as you handle the day's setbacks and frustrations? Or do they see you put yourself down? Do you often mention the weight you need to lose? Do you panic about the wrinkles that are accumulating? Or do you radiate a sense of self-worth and peace with what is? They are watching. *We* teach our children how to generate their own self-compassion.

2. Practice Gratitude

We must protect ourselves from falling into the comparison trap and the best way to do that is to practice gratitude. That's right, 10 minutes a day, in your mind, in your journal, in your phone, write the things you are grateful for. That bright blue sky, the singing birds, the sweet smell of your kids' hair, the color of your nails. Get creative and go wild. The drive to get what we think we deserve will only fuel discontent with what we have. This unhealthy obsession will steer us away from our true selves and who we were meant to be. Instead of chasing what someone else has in an attempt to prove your worth, nurture and grow what is true for you and your unique identity. Then, surround yourself with safe people, those who love you for who you are, not for the image you portray. The more people know who we really are, the more they will be drawn to us. We have enough fake in this modern world. Be real. Be you.

The truth is, you may still compare yourself to others at times. Maybe you won't even realize it, but before you know it, you will be consumed with jealousy. In those moments, fight your natural tendency to covet. Instead, run toward and encourage the very people you are tempted to envy. Be grateful for their gifts, what you admire about them, and the talents and beauty they bring to this world. It is so much better to encourage others than to beat up on yourself. You will feel better. And use yourself, not others, as your benchmark. Learn to admire qualities in other people without questioning your own value and worth.

Listen to me closely. Other people's attributes and gifts do not lessen your value. The apostle Paul described the early church as one body with many parts. Each part had a role to play, and one member was not more important than another: "But in fact God has placed the parts in the body, every one of them, just as he wanted them to be. If they were all one part, where would the body be? As it is, there are many parts, but one body" (1 Cor. 12:18-20). If you are a foot, stop comparing yourself to the ear. Don't despise the part you are equipped to play. No matter your role, you are uniquely valuable, and God assigns your value, which cannot be earned or lost. So, stop your striving and the jockeying for position. You are not valuable because of the car you drive or the college you graduated from or the social groups you hang out with. You are valuable because you are his. He created you, and you are "fearfully and wonderfully made" (Ps. 139:14).

Start living your story. You are worthy right now, exactly as you are. Coco Chanel once said, "Beauty begins the moment you decide to be yourself." This is true because beauty comes out of inner confidence and inner peace. Wear it. Own it. Flaws and all. They make you beautiful.

Reflection Questions:

1. How much time and energy do you spend focusing on others' lives?

2. In what ways do you model self-compassion for your children? What do they witness in your life that encourages them to extend grace to themselves?

3. What would allow you to let go of comparison, discontentment, and jealousy and instead embrace the true, authentic you?

4. Right now make a list of all the things others have said they love about you. Say three of them to yourself in the morning and evening. Write them down in your journal daily.

New Insight:

_____

_____

_____

_____

_____

_____

_____

_____

_____

_____

_____

_____

Myth 3

It Is Too Late to Find My Purpose

The two most important days in your life are the day you are born and the day you find out why.

—MARK TWAIN

Do you feel like you are missing something in your life, like you are going through the motions without living a life of purpose? You want more. You need more. But you can't figure out what it could be. You don't quite know how to get there.

Guess what? You *are* created for more. You have a purpose, and as long as you are not sure what it is, we are robbed of your brilliance.

Maybe you just graduated from college, but you don't know what's next. Perhaps you're a new mother, grateful to have your child, yet longing to make a difference in the larger world as well. Maybe you have been through the diaper trenches and the teenage roller-coaster and your kids are launched. Now what? Who are

> When we live life on purpose, everything falls into place.

you, after you've put life on hold for so long? Perhaps you're the corporate woman. You've played the game and it's worked for you; you're meeting your corporate goals, yet you still feel empty. You are not quite sure why, but you just can't shake the feeling that something different is out there for you.

When we live life on purpose, everything falls into place. We are motivated, fulfilled, and focused. What we focus on is what we become. When we aren't living on purpose, we are spinning in circles without direction.

Lisa's Story: A Brave Roadmap to Passion Meets Purpose

Lisa was a client who came to me because she felt empty inside. She had a great job and a lovely family. Others would say she had a "perfect" life. As we set goals for our work together, Lisa wasn't even sure what she wanted to work on. Her kids were grown and didn't need her daily anymore. Her job paid well, so she didn't have the desire to leave, yet she went to work each day feeling empty. She felt her job as an accountant could easily be done by someone else while she had a desire to impact lives directly. She just wasn't sure how. In addition, Lisa had bought the lie that it was too late to figure out her purpose or change tracks. She didn't believe she could still be used to create amazing things.

We began by searching for Lisa's passions. What did she love? What did she dislike? We explored circumstances that made her feel alive and energized and things that made her feel like she was down and uninterested.

In exploring her passions, Lisa said she loved working outside in nature, in the garden or her yard. She loved attending theater productions, listening to classical music, and watching SEC football games. Lisa was also passionate about volunteering with the abuse-recovery women's ministry at her church; it was fulfilling to know she could support and encourage women walking through difficult times.

When I asked Lisa what she would do if she had all of the resources she needed and knew she couldn't fail, she instantly replied that she would start a recovery house for these women so that they could get back on their feet. When I asked why, she shared that she witnessed her own mother struggle in many unhealthy relationships. She always wondered what her mom could have accomplished if she had a safety net.

We were getting to the heart of Lisa's passions, which helped us define her purpose. Once we discovered her passions, we were able to move into action. What was getting in the way of moving toward her biggest dream: opening a women's recovery house? Was it negative self-talk? Doubt? Lack of time? Lack of balance?

In Lisa's case, it was a little bit of everything. When reflecting on her obstacles, she determined they were mostly self-imposed. She had the resources she needed, as well as the time. Her husband would be supportive of any venture she attempted. Lisa concluded that *she just didn't believe she could do it.*

Ahhh . . . there it is. I am amazed each time I see a new example of how thoroughly self-doubt sabotages us and keeps. Us. Stuck. In my mind, I thought, "Why, Lisa? Why don't you think you can do it?" I was sitting across from a competent, goal-driven, intelligent woman. Isn't it interesting how our own impression of ourselves is so vastly different from other people's image of us? After some exploration, we uncovered it. No one in her life ever told her she could. No one ever gave her permission to dream big, set goals, and aim for the sky.

Lisa also shared that part of her felt guilty for dreaming big when she watched her mother struggle just to stay afloat emotionally and financially. To avoid making her mom uncomfortable, she unconsciously decided to stay small.

After challenging her false beliefs, Lisa was slowly able to give herself permission to step out in fresh, exciting ways. She researched how to meet the needs of women fleeing abusive homes. She met with her church to see if there would be a way to expand their mission to accommodate more people. Lisa met with a loan officer to see if she could qualify for a loan that would allow her to afford a small house for temporary occupancy. She networked with other nonprofits in the area to learn how they ran their agencies. I could hardly keep up with all of the action she was boldly taking. It was incredible to watch.

That is what happens, my friends, when we live a life of purpose motivated by passion. The fog clears; our vision is clear; and we are suddenly imbued with enormous amounts of energy.

Truth 1: It Is Never Too Late to Find Your Purpose

Our purpose becomes clearer throughout life's journey. Each step clarifies our gifts and passions as we observe the impact our contributions have on others and learn from the impact others have on us. We gain wisdom as we age, becoming more comfortable in our identity. In a sense, we just get better with time. Thus, it is never too late to find your purpose. Consider individuals who have continued to make a tremendous impact into later life; for example, Mother Theresa worked into her eighties, serving and loving others.

You don't retire from purpose; rather, it changes and evolves your entire life. Sometimes, your later years are the best time to identify why you are here. Once the chaos and daily grind of raising kiddos is over, you experience a quiet vacuum that might be the environment you need to cultivate and create your mission.

Truth 2: Finding Your Purpose Is a Journey

Sadly, it's not as easy as waking up one morning to find a note under your pillow defining your purpose. Instead, you find your purpose through work, exploration, and self-study. You must reflect on what you need more of and what you need less of. Take time to analyze the components of your life if you want to move into a more productive and purposeful space.

This work must be intentional. Anyone can do it, but it won't just happen. Schedule time to evaluate, plan, pray, and dream. Talk to trusted others, but remember that no one else can tell you your purpose. You alone know the desires of your heart and the activities that make you feel most energetic.

Do This Instead: Work Towards Passion

1. Clarify Your Values and Passions

Find what drives you. What situations in the world keep you up at night? Where do you want to see justice and change? What can you never get enough of? You may ultimately choose to work with a coach in self-exploration, but you can begin by considering the questions under "Clarifying Values" and "Purpose Questionnaire" in the appendix.

2. Cast Your Vision

Proverbs 29:18 says, "Where there is no vision, the people perish." In other words, without clarifying your vision for the future, you will wander aimlessly; your sense of purpose will wither, and you may find yourself feeling depressed.

So, how do you cast a vision for your best life? Knowing your values helps you cast a vision. What do you want? What opportunities do you have that you are not taking advantage of?

What obstacles could get in your way? Negative self-talk? Doubt imposed by others? Poor time management?

Consider capturing your thoughts in a vision statement, a brief declaration of the journey you are on and the end result you desire. Return to this statement during moments when doubt creeps in or setbacks interrupt. Struggle and detours are part of any epic journey, but a vision statement is your map, your true north during those trying seasons.

3. Act

Move! Try things out. Make mistakes. Roll up your sleeves and get messy. Fail forward. Your attempts don't have to be perfect. You just have to try.

As you act, your purpose will become clearer. You will feel energized because you are making progress, getting closer and closer to your goals. Before you know it, you are on mission and unstoppable!

Reflection Questions:

1. In what areas are you spinning your wheels without gaining traction?
2. What is your purpose? What inspires you to get up each day?
3. If you don't have a clearly defined purpose, ask, what *don't* I want? Eliminating the things that do not bring joy and fulfillment is a good place to start.
4. What would you do if you had all of the resources you needed and knew you couldn't fail?

New Insight:

Myth 4

If I Feel That Way, It Must Be True

Some of the worst things in my life never happened.
–MARK TWAIN

Ladies, we must capture our feelings. I get it. It is hard. I am a feeler. On the scale of feeling versus thinking, I am a full feeler. If you are familiar with personality assessments, imagine the highest score for feeler. That's me; let there be no room for confusion.

However, my feeling something is true doesn't make it true. Did you catch that? Let me say it another way: our feelings are not always facts. Ouch. I know. It seems like they are. I am still convincing myself—though my mind knows it's true. And, because it's true, I must pass this wisdom along to you, dear reader. Feelings aren't facts, and when you confuse them for solid truth, they get between you and your best life.

Our most powerful negative feelings are usually brought on by negative self-talk, that broken record of doubt and less-than that plays in our mind during the down times. Negative self-talk hijacks our happiness and joy. It impacts our self-esteem. It makes us feel miserable and shuts us down. If we don't learn to put feelings in proper perspective, we will inevitably believe our negative feelings are the way life is, not just the way we are seeing it.

Katherine's Story: Redefining an Old Belief

A few years ago, I was seeing a client named Katherine. Katherine came to our sessions upset about how people treated her. Everywhere she went, she ran into people who "didn't like her": the cashier in the checkout line; the instructor at her barre class; her neighbors who ignored her when she yelled hello; her son's fifth grade teacher. Should I go on? I think you get it.

Once, Katherine was at the movies with a friend. After the movie ended, they were standing near the top of the stairs catching up. While standing there, another movie let out and people streamed toward them and down the stairs. Katherine said she noticed an acquaintance walking toward her and got ready to say hi. When the acquaintance walked by without even looking at her, Katherine felt snubbed. She turned to her friend and said, "I knew she didn't like me."

Wow! What a gross assumption and a quick way to feel horrible. As a therapist, I didn't even know where to go with this. I couldn't believe how quickly Katherine jumped to conclusions and decided that just because she felt like this woman might not like her, then it must be true.

I questioned her gently as her defenses were clearly up. "How do we know she doesn't like you?" I asked cautiously.

"Well, she didn't say hello to me," she replied.

"Is there any possible chance she didn't see you?" I inquired gently.

Katherine sat for a moment in thought. I could see she was wrestling with this question. It was important for her to be right. It was important for her to prove her point, but the evidence wasn't there. She couldn't back it up.

"Well, it is possible she didn't see me," she said reluctantly. "In fact, when I mentioned it to my friend, she immediately responded that the woman didn't even see me."

"Oh, so you think she might not have even *seen* you?" I asked.

"I actually don't think she did. I think she was looking at the stairs, making sure she didn't trip."

Do you see what just happened? We went from Katherine's assumption (Brené Brown calls this "the story we are telling ourselves") that this acquaintance didn't like her and was snubbing her to the possibility that this woman didn't even see her. With that small shift, she moved from feeling rejected to feeling neutral about their interaction.

Just because Katherine *felt* this woman didn't like her, her assumption didn't make it true. In therapy, we call these unfounded assumptions cognitive distortions. Because of our fears and insecurities, we magnify a situation and jump to the worst conclusion. When we let our feelings lead the way, we will cling to our distortions and spend much of the day feeling worthless and stuck—all because of our flawed interpretation of an event. We need *truth* to combat the negative, automatic thoughts that produce feelings of shame and inadequacy.

Truth 1: Feelings Are Not a Truth Compass

How often do we jump to conclusions? I know I do, and I see it in others, too: in politics, in friendships, in families. We see things through a particular lens, which is formed by our background and beliefs. We tell ourselves a distorted, ill-informed version of what happened but spin it as *objective fact*. Without realizing it, we catastrophize and let *subjective story* hijack the truth. We let feelings pull us to one side of the issue, and we shut down other points of view.

We keep ourselves from victory and joy by playing negative feelings on a continuous loop in our mind. We feel hurt or upset, and we construct an emotionally charged script that, over time, we believe. But, be careful. Just because you feel she left you out on purpose doesn't make it true. Just because your daughter had her feelings hurt by a friend doesn't mean the friend is mean. Just because you parent differently than your sister doesn't mean your sister is a bad parent. Do you see where I am going here?

> We see things through a particular lens, which is formed by our background and beliefs.

Our *mind-set* is crucial. If we don't notice our negative emotions and the associated catastrophized assumptions, we lose power over our reactions. You see, our thoughts and feelings shape our actions and reactions. It is crucial that we get to the root of the issue and decide the weight we will give to the feeling-infused thoughts shaping our perception. Only then can we determine the appropriate response.

Truth 2: The Battle Happens in the "Mind"-Field

You see, a wide-open canyon of a space exists between something that happens (A: an activating event) and how we handle it (D: what you do about it/ your response).

Activating Event   Do About It

That open space is a minefield (or, as I like to call it, a *mindfield)*, and the battle is fierce. The mindfield is the space between what happens and how we respond.

This is where the lies seep in and take over. They can sound like this: "I knew she didn't like me"; "I always fail"; "I am not important enough"; "I am not pretty enough"; "Why do I even try? Nothing ever works out for me!" Or how about this one: "I don't matter"?

Look at the chart below as I give you an illustration. This chart was shared with me by Dr. Terry Casey, licensed psychologist and faculty at Lipscomb University, as a variation of Rational Emotive Behavioral Therapy, created by Albert Ellis.

Mindfield

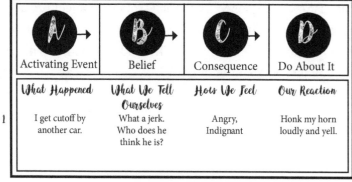

	Activating Event	Belief	Consequence	Do About It
	What Happened	What We Tell Ourselves	How We Feel	Our Reaction
Scenario 1	I get cutoff by another car.	What a jerk. Who does he think he is?	Angry, Indignant	Honk my horn loudly and yell.

Imagine you are driving down the road and get cut off by another car ("activating event," column A). How do you feel when you get cut off by that car ("consequence," column C)? Angry? How do you react (what you "do about it," column D)? Do you yell, honk your horn, or give the driver a not-so-nice hand gesture?

Now let's look at what you are telling yourself at that moment (your "belief," column B). You may be thinking, "What a jerk! Who does he think he is?"

The problem we get ourselves into is this: we jump to conclusions without evidence or truth. We make up stories in our mind about how things are, without really knowing the objective reality of a situation. And, the stories we are making up are shaped by our mood, bias, temperament, and ...*feelings.*

Okay. Now, let's rework this scenario, but this time, we have to filter our belief through the grid of objective evidence. It might look like this: The same activating event happens, you get cut off by a car. But, instead of jumping to conclusions about the driver, his character, and his intentions, we filter the event through *evidence and truth.* Do we have evidence this driver is a jerk? No. Do we know he was trying to disrespect us? No. Perhaps he was on his way to the hospital or late to a job interview. You might have been in his blind spot.

How do you feel now when you consider getting cut off by that car ("consequence," column C)? Is your anger replaced with a more neutral feeling? How do you react to that incident now (what you "do about it," column D)? Instead of reacting with volatility, do you just go about your day?

Mindfield

Activating Event	Belief	Consequence	Do About It
What Happened	**What We Tell Ourselves**	**How We Feel**	**Our Reaction**
Scenario 1 Katherine feels ignored by a friend.	This always happens to me, no one else.	Rejected, hurt, lonely.	Build up walls with people so I don't get hurt.
Scenario 2 Katherine feels ignored by a friend.	FILTER THROUGH TRUTH OR EVIDENCE: Maybe she didn't see me.	Neutral	Go about my day.

Isn't it fascinating that our stories (our thoughts) have power over our feelings and actions? In the mindfield, we need to notice our false belief, the automatic thought that pops into our head. The realm of thought, which forms our beliefs, is where change happens. Let's filter Katherine's case through the same ABCD chart:

Mindfield

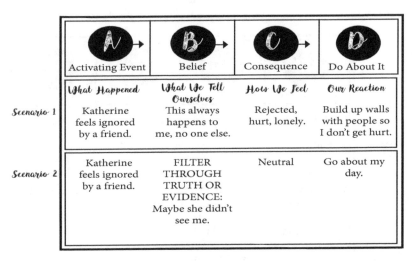

	Activating Event	Belief	Consequence	Do About It
	What Happened	What We Tell Ourselves	How We Feel	Our Reaction
Scenario 1	Katherine feels ignored by a friend.	This always happens to me, no one else.	Rejected, hurt, lonely.	Build up walls with people so I don't get hurt.
Scenario 2	Katherine feels ignored by a friend.	FILTER THROUGH TRUTH OR EVIDENCE: Maybe she didn't see me.	Neutral	Go about my day.

What about a scenario in which we are dealing with internal shame?

Mindfield

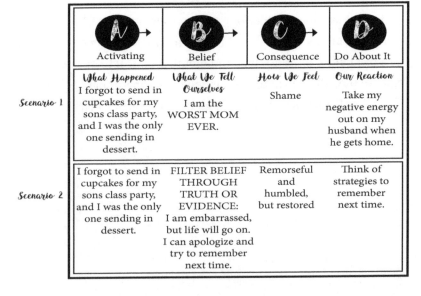

	Activating	Belief	Consequence	Do About It
	What Happened	What We Tell Ourselves	How We Feel	Our Reaction
Scenario 1	I forgot to send in cupcakes for my sons class party, and I was the only one sending in dessert.	I am the WORST MOM EVER.	Shame	Take my negative energy out on my husband when he gets home.
Scenario 2	I forgot to send in cupcakes for my sons class party, and I was the only one sending in dessert.	FILTER BELIEF THROUGH TRUTH OR EVIDENCE: I am embarrassed, but life will go on. I can apologize and try to remember next time.	Remorseful and humbled, but restored	Think of strategies to remember next time.

As you can see, the problem with the mindfield is that the negative stories we tell ourselves impact our feelings, which then shape our actions. When we react emotionally (column D) we create a new activating event (column A) that we now must deal with. Before long, we are in a negative thought spiral: negative thought, negative emotion, negative action, negative thought, negative emotion, negative action. We experience life from a different place when we are in a negative-talk spiral (and it is *not* good). Could we also create an upward spiral if our thoughts are positive? Yes. That is the wonderful thing. We *do* have the ability to spawn a positive spiral.

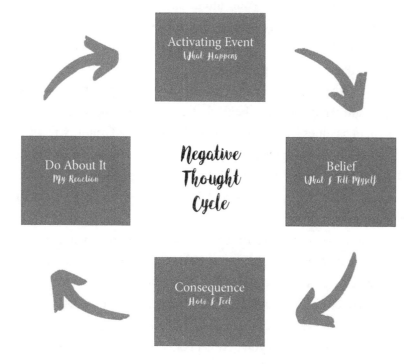

Ladies, do you notice that this is all from within? Our self-talk—not the other person—is the truly dangerous element. The other person isn't doing a thing. This battle is internal. Nobody tells us to think this way. We are doing this to ourselves, and it is so easy to point fingers at others.

Do This Instead: Work Towards Understanding

1. Notice Self-Sabotaging Thoughts

Stop. Observe your feelings and follow the trail back to the thoughts that produced them. What is it you are really feeling? Maybe you feel excited, joyful, and confident because you've been feeding your mind uplifting messages. Yay, you!

But what if you are hurt, angry, lonely, or sad? Those feelings are valid and deserve your attention. Stuffing them down or denying them will only prolong the misery. Instead, get curious. Ask yourself, "What am I thinking and believing to produce or prolong these unsettling feelings?"

Your feelings—and the thoughts that support them—are important. They are also helpful *if* you are willing to listen and use them as clues, warning signs, and indicators. Crummy feelings signal crummy thoughts and beliefs. Where did the self-sabotaging thought patterns come from? Important figures in childhood? Friends who let you down? Past failures or embarrassing memories? Comparison?

Before you can move forward, you have to know what you are feeling and then work to understand your emotions' connection to your thoughts. If you grew up being told you had to stuff your negative feelings and maintain a sunny façade to receive love, it may be difficult for you to get in touch with the feelings society labels as "bad." But, I encourage you to reflect on and validate each feeling as an important step toward dismantling self-sabotaging thoughts.

2. Filter Thoughts through Evidence and Truth

Once you've identified your core thoughts and beliefs, the next step is to filter them through the grid of evidence and truth. In other words, ask, "What am I telling myself, and is it true? What if I look for *evidence* and *truth* before I allow feelings to take over?" Did Katherine use factual evidence to decide whether her acquaintance liked her? Would her feelings and, ultimately, her response have changed if she had slowed down to consider the evidence?

We can't move into the amazing lives we are called to live when we are stuck in a warped and distorted mindfield of unevaluated negative feeling. That space robs us of joy and gratitude and keeps us stuck.

3. Examine the Fruit of Your Thoughts

Once you have captured your thoughts, we want to honor God with them (2 Cor. 10:5). Do we honor God when we put ourself down? Is it pleasing to God when you insult his creation (*you*)? Notice how negative thoughts move you away from his plan for your life and limit you from doing the work you are meant to do. Our thoughts are always producing *something*. Are yours lifting you up or bringing you down? Are they producing delicious and nourishing fruit or sowing seeds of sadness? I encourage you to use the "Blank ABCD Chart" I've provided in the appendix as you work through your own self-sabotaging thoughts.

Reflection Questions:

1. In what situations do you jump to conclusions and believe your feelings represent truth, rather than considering the facts?

2. How can you capture self-sabotaging thoughts and filter them through evidence and truth?
3. Which relationships would flourish if you filtered feelings through evidence and truth?

New Insight: _____

_____

_____

_____

_____

_____

_____

_____

_____

_____

_____

_____

_____

Myth 5

My Kids Define Who I Am

Parents can only give good advice or put them on the right paths, but the final forming of a person's character lies in their own hands.

—ANNE FRANK

This myth generates compassion in me for moms who struggle with keeping motherhood and parenting in proper perspective. It is heartbreaking to watch women stay stuck in the lie that their kids' successes or failures define their personal worth. And, I would be inauthentic if I didn't acknowledge that I have to keep this in check myself.

Kid comparison is quite severe in today's world where envy and unworthiness is fueled by social media. But, truly, I think this problem has been around for a while. I don't remember my mother feeling validated by my accomplishments or feeling embarrassed by my failures, but I am sure other moms of that era did. And the children whose mothers looked to them for identity likely learned to put their expectations on their own children and so on. Generational patterns run strong, folks.

Karen's Story: Discovering a New Bank of Self-Worth

Karen was a forty-five-year-old mother of three. Her oldest daughter, Katie, was about to go to college. Her middle daughter, Bethany, was a freshman in high school, and her son, Ben, was in sixth grade.

Karen came to me because Katie was struggling, and she was trying to process her emotions and figure out how to help her daughter. Katie had recently been in trouble for "juuling" at school, and shared that her grades were slipping as well. It was clear from Karen's concern that this was new territory for her, and it was disconcerting.

Discussing her daughter's challenges, Karen expressed fear that others would judge her as a bad parent. She was also concerned about her ninth-grade daughter, Bethany, who seemed to be withdrawing. Her grades were slipping as well, and Karen couldn't figure out why. A friend recently asked Karen if Bethany was on the honor roll, and Karen felt shame when she had to answer no. What would people think of her for raising two daughters who weren't star students?

Karen also worried that Bethany didn't have any friends at school and wasn't invited to the popular girls' parties. Karen believed her life and her daughter's would be better if only Bethany were popular like her older sister, Katie. She reluctantly shared her worries that people might judge her because her daughter was not popular.

In contrast, Karen beamed when she talked about Ben, an all-star athlete on a travel team for both basketball and baseball. She said that, on average, they were gone three weekends a month attending tournaments all around the region and sometimes all around the country. They spent unimaginable amounts of money on Ben's sports because she was certain he would get a sports scholarship. She acknowledged that her girls might get less attention, but she believed they knew how important Ben's sports were for his future.

Karen confessed that their household felt like it was falling apart. They rarely ate together as a family because Ben's baseball practices and games were in the evening. She left the girls and her husband to fend for themselves. Ben was so busy with sports that Karen had taken it upon herself to do his homework so he would be able to keep straight As. Her husband told her it was ridiculous for her to do Ben's work, but she didn't listen. The cost of Ben giving up his starting position on the basketball team seemed unimaginable to Karen. She couldn't let go of the pride she felt having a star athlete and an apparent star student.

Karen remembered what it felt like when she tried out for the cheerleading squad and didn't make it. Memories surfaced of her friends making the cut and squealing together as they looked at the posted cheerleading list. She was with them, but her name wasn't on the list. She felt invisible, a complete outsider standing alone. Karen never wanted to feel like an outsider again.

Friends, myth 5 is played out over and over again, yet Karen—and many other moms—can't see that it is untrue. Karen was miserable because she was getting her worth from and finding her identity in her children, specifically their performances. She needed them to perform and make the cut because if they didn't, she'd be invisible—no better than that day in high school when she was cut from the squad.

> Why do we manipulate our kids' lives so that we can feel better about our own?

Why do parents buy the lie that they can heal personal wounds through their kids? Why do we manipulate our kids' lives so that we can feel better about our own? The truth is, it's quite easy to get caught up in our kids and their success. Controlling their success and ensuring they never fail can look like loving parenting, but is it?

Truth 1: Only You Can Heal Your Story

Our kids are not here to heal our wounds. They are not created to take care of the brokenness we felt growing up. If you are looking to that precious little angel or that hormonal teenager to repair your hurt, you must recognize it is not their job. When we put that responsibility on them, we are creating reasons for them to be in therapy as adults. They will experience crushing anxiety when they realize how desperate you are for them to succeed. They may also have a hard time forming an authentic identity as they are doing what you expect instead of what makes them come alive.

> Our kids are not here to heal our wounds.

If you were picked last at the dance, is it important for your daughter to be popular so she doesn't experience the same feeling? If you were overweight, do you put pressure on your daughter to be skinny? If you didn't make the cheer squad, is it important that your daughter makes it, even if she doesn't feel comfortable with that crowd or that activity?

If your child gets a C, do you come unglued? Do you worry what people will think if he doesn't make it into a prestigious college? Do you get a grade on his grades? Are you the parent at the baseball game who insists your son play second base? If he is in the game but doesn't play well, are you humiliated? During the game, are you the parent yelling out ways he could play better? Do you acknowledge all the ways your son messed up a play so other parents will know you are aware of his failure? Ouch. Yes. Parents do that. Visit any Little League baseball field in your town to see countless adults reliving their youth through their kids. Parents routinely shame their kids, displacing part of the humiliation they feel over the child's performance.

None of us like to see our children walk through difficult times, but the question is, *do their difficult times bring up our difficult times?* And, if so, how do we look inward

> Do their difficult times bring up our difficult times?

and do our own work, or do we pressure them to get it right so we can feel vindicated for past personal failures?

Truth 2: Your Kids Are Their Own Beautiful Beings

We must be our own person, and we must let our child be himself, too. At some point in time I heard this lack of differentiation refered to as "E.T. Syndrome." In case you haven't seen the 1982 movie *E.T. the Extra-Terrestrial* by Steven Spielberg, it is about an alien who gets stuck on earth and is cared for by a boy named Elliot. The two of them become best friends and develop a supernatural connection with each other. So much so, that at the end of the movie when E.T.'s health begins to diminish, Elliott begins fading, too. Elliott absorbs E.T.'s illness and emotions as his own; no distinction remains between the two. Luckily, E.T. and Elliot pull through—in case you were concerned.

As women, we can reflect the emotions and level of well-being our children experience. Imagine your daughter comes home from school hurt by the way someone treated her. Immediately, *you* are hurt. Her pain becomes your pain. With E.T. Syndrome, you want to find that mean girl and put her in her place. You text her mom (because calling would be too confrontational) and let her know that her daughter needs to fix her behavior. You are justified in doing so because your daughter was hurt. And you were hurt. You will manage this situation and all future encounters to make sure she is never hurt again.

It can look like this, too. Your son didn't make the school basketball team. He is devastated. It is as if *you* didn't make the school team. You are devastated. And angry. So, you call the school to let them know the evaluations weren't fair. You tell them they made a mistake. Yes, you become *that* parent. You can't bear the idea of your son being disappointed. You take on the pain and micromanage the situation until you can both feel okay.

Of course you are going to be sad when your kids walk through disappointment. You love your children with all of your heart and want the best for them. The challenge comes when you go into the hurt and take it as your own. Instead, we must differentiate and become a healthy source of *outside* support. Let them know we are there, a refuge for them to rest in, offering solace to help them deal with their pain, but it is essential that they learn how to handle disappointment. If we rush in to erase the pain, they may grow up stuffing negative feelings or using poor coping tools to deal with them.

Feelings are guideposts. We want to teach our kids how to notice them and then use them to discern the best next step. It is okay to feel disappointment. It is okay to be sad, hurt, angry, or afraid. Feelings are part of the human experience. Our discomfort with hard feelings teaches kids that failure, pain, and disappointment are intolerable. Scrambling to make everything feel better fast is sending the signal that they must be perfect to avoid negative feelings. And, if those unpleasant feelings do come, they must quickly find someone else to blame or make it right.

Rather, it is our job to teach them what to do with hard feelings. We must demonstrate how to use feelings for growth and understanding. Emotions are gifts to learn from. It has been said,

"Prepare the child for the road, not the road for the child." If we don't let our kids experience pain, we rob them of resilience. They need to learn how to fall and get back up. They need to learn how to handle not making the team and see that life will go on and everything will be okay. It really will.

It is not likely that your child will get a college sports scholarship, and neither will mine. (I am not trying to be a downer; just look at the statistics.) What *is* likely is that they will encounter a lifetime of adversity, disappointments, heartache, setbacks, failures, and challenges. They need to know you are right there next to them, cheering them on but not fixing or micromanaging. Show them you believe in their ability to get back up and persevere.

Truth 3: You Are More Than *Just* a Mother

We can become so consumed with motherhood that we lose who we are as an individual. Don't misunderstand me. *Yes*, your kids are important. Absolutely. They need unconditional love and attention, and when they are young, they need lots of it. But, motherhood is not your identity. You are not one dimensional, and you cannot suppress passions, hobbies, and interests if you want to live versus survive.

Maybe it has been a while since you considered your passions. Perhaps it is time to prioritize what you love, what you want more of, and what makes you feel alive. You have unique gifts, strengths, and abilities that set you apart. What are they? What would you do if you had all of the resources you needed and knew you couldn't fail?

Taking care of yourself is not selfish. Even Jesus knew when he needed to be alone to spend time with his Father. He separated himself to recharge, regroup, and focus on his mission. One of the greatest gifts you can give your kids is to demonstrate self-care and show them how to cultivate their passions by spending time on your own. We can't give from an empty cup.

Do This Instead: Work Towards Affirmation

1. Be Their Safe Refuge

Friends, I know. We can't help but be impacted when we watch our kiddos suffer, but we can choose to step back and let their experiences be theirs. They need you to be someone with whom they can process feelings—not someone equally consumed by the feeling. Remember, they aren't going to share their concerns if they think you can't handle it or will become upset.

Though you will naturally have feelings about what they share, it is important to be present and supportive of your child and then process your emotions with someone else. As they are growing, you can share your feelings with your spouse, a close friend, your small group, or a therapist. Do not inflict your pain and disappointment on your child. Your feelings are too much for them to carry. Children should never feel as if they have to emotionally regulate their parents. It is our job to teach them how to organize their own feelings, not manage ours. We need to be stronger, braver, and wiser so they can feel secure in order to find their place in this world.

2. Fill Your Own Cup

Create space and self-care for you. Recharge through solitude or with friends. Take a class, join a club, or train for a race. Find a counselor where you can process anything that is holding you back. Whatever makes you feel alive and energized, do it. We can't be there for our families when we are running empty. I know that in different seasons of life, this is often easier said than done. I get it. But challenge yourself to try it, even for an hour, and see if you return to your family with renewed energy and proper perspective.

Reflection Questions:

1.   In what areas do you take on more responsibility than you should with your children? Why do you feel the need to intervene?
2.   Can you separate your feelings and problems from your kids' feelings and problems?
3.   In what ways can you increase your sense of purpose—apart from your kids—and practice better self-care?

New Insight:

_____

_____

_____

_____

_____

_____

_____

_____

_____

_____

_____

Myth 6

It Is Not Okay to Say No

The first thing you need to know is that the person who is angry at you
for setting boundaries is the one with the problem.
–DRS. HENRY CLOUD AND JOHN TOWNSEND

When I began my life coaching certification training program in 2008, I was running ragged. My husband was in the Navy and deployed in Iraq for a year. I was holding everything together at home with a four- and six-year-old. The days were long and exhausting. The kids missed their dad desperately and couldn't quite make sense of his lack of presence. It was heartbreaking to watch their disappointment and sadness as they coped with his absence.

Our daughter, Keilah, had the most difficult time. She was in first grade, and though I didn't realize it, she concluded that I had sent Dad away and "let" him go serve our country. She didn't understand it was his job and he couldn't say no. At school, other kids were talking about the war in Iraq and discussing horror stories that they had somehow been exposed to. She heard these stories and assumed that her dad would not make it home. Luke was four at the time, and while he missed his dad terribly, he didn't quite process the risks associated with the assignment.

Not only was I stretched at home and dealing with my own loneliness, but I was also overcommitted in our community. I was saying yes to every committee that requested my participation. I was on school boards, military boards, and neighborhood boards. I was bringing meals to friends and cookies to school. I was also serving at church.

For some reason, it seemed the perfect time to go back to school for my life coaching certification and then for my master's in counseling. In all honesty, I am not sure what I was thinking. God knew, though. He used that opportunity to shine a light on the way I was living my life. Through my coaching training, my bad habit of saying yes became crystal clear. I was able to see, with 20/20 vision, my lack of boundaries.

I was saying yes to anything that came my way in an attempt to fit in or feel connected. And the thing is, they were mostly things that I really wanted to do; I just didn't have enough hours in the day to get it all done. Can you relate?

I admit that, as a recovering people pleaser, I really struggle with saying no. I want to make others happy and avoid disappointing anyone, especially those I love. However, now I can recognize when I get into that people-pleasing space and am saying yes when I ought not. I get a queasy feeling in my stomach. My back tenses up, and my shoulders tighten. I've learned to listen to my body and can now pull back when I am saying yes but need to say no.

Sarah's Story: Finding Common Connection Ground

When I first met Sarah, she was excited to be newly married. Most of her friends had already been to the altar, and she had been concerned about finding someone special to share her life with.

Their marriage began beautifully, as every couple would hope for. They quickly welcomed their first child and were adjusting to family life. Before long, though, challenges set in as they dealt with extended family.

Sarah grew up in a close-knit family. They lived in the same town, celebrated most holidays together, and loved any chance to spend time together. Sarah's husband, Scott, on the other hand, grew up in a family that was somewhat disconnected. They saw each other a few times a year and rarely spoke on the phone. He wasn't close to his siblings, and after his dad left home when he was twelve, he hardly maintained a relationship with him.

Sarah shared in session one day that she and Scott were having arguments over family involvement. Scott felt Sarah's family was too enmeshed in their time and decisions. He felt pressure from Sarah's parents to include them in most family events and was extremely resentful when they wanted a voice in the new baby's name selection. In addition, he was particularly bothered by the way her parents let themselves in at Sarah and Scott's without notice, arriving unannounced.

Sarah felt hurt that Scott didn't love her family as much as she did. She explained his feelings by saying he must feel jealous of her family's love for each other. Sarah was hurt that his parents hardly showed any interest in the baby; she resented his mother's reluctance to visit.

Two years into marriage, trouble was brewing on the home front. The honeymoon faded as their relationship faced boundary challenges. Can you see how the boundaries between Sarah and Scott's families of origin are vastly different?

The Truth about Healthy Boundaries

Imagine you have your own castle, a grand fortress in the middle of a valley with flowers and hills surrounding it. Brightly colored flags fly high from the top of the castle, representing your family crest. The entrance is protected by a large mote filled with ferocious alligators. You also have soldiers standing on top of the tower, ensuring the castle will remain safe and protected.

Now, imagine you have all this protection (the alligators and the soldiers), but you also have a major flaw. You have lowered the drawbridge and left it open, having been told that closing the drawbridge would be selfish. You have allowed invaders to come in and out as they please without any consequences. You have allowed people to take advantage of the open drawbridge, and, in some way, they have physically or emotionally destroyed your castle.

Or imagine the opposite scenario. You have this beautiful castle, full of artwork, rooms for guests, and an overflowing kitchen. But because of past hurts, or maybe because of what you were taught, you have left the drawbridge up and sealed. You have kept it closed and have refused to open it. You think the world is not safe. Or you have been hurt beyond imagination, and it is just too scary to risk letting anyone in. So, you sit alone in your castle, wondering what you might be missing beyond the walls, wondering how it would feel to be seen and connected.

Both scenarios are harmful. On one end of the spectrum, when we keep our drawbridge down and don't have any personal limits, we risk letting others take advantage of us and violate our space. On the other end of the spectrum, when we keep the drawbridge up, we miss out on deep, authentic connection with others and are alone. Ideally, we are taught by our parents how to open and close the drawbridge and adjust our boundaries as needed. We are shown how to let the good in and wisely keep the harmful out.

Unfortunately, not all of us have the opportunity to learn proper boundaries from emotionally healthy parents. But that doesn't mean it is too late. We can all learn healthy boundaries. We can learn to say yes when it is life-giving for both parties. And, conversely, we can say no as an appropriate way to take back proper control of our life.

Truth 1: No.

Raise your hand if you have heard, "The phrase 'no' is a sentence?" Many of us cringe at saying no, as if it is a bad word, as if it is mean. We go to great lengths to avoid no. For some, it is because we were raised in an environment where we learned that no was disagreeable and difficult and, therefore, bad. Shame and punishment may have followed the perceived disrespect and disobedience of not going along. Or maybe the punishment wasn't overt. Maybe you received a passive-aggressive guilt trip as loved ones communicated how hurt or disappointed they were by your no.

Well, today, I am giving you permission. I am giving you complete freedom and power to say no when you need to. Ideally, we are saying no clearly and firmly but with love and respect, acknowledging the legitimacy of our own needs. We are agreeing others' needs are important while also remembering that not every need is ours to fill. We can't give until we are depleted and shouldn't give out of compunction. If we can't say yes with a joyful and ready spirit, then we should at least consider saying no. Why are you hesitating? Get curious about your reluctance and lean into what is true for you in that moment. While being agreeable can be helpful in many circumstances, we have to find our voice to say no when needed. Sometimes no is the only way to stay healthy and respect our personal boundaries.

Truth 2: Others' Disappointments Are Theirs to Own

Feelings are just feelings. They pass. No feeling is permanent. It is okay to be disappointed for a moment or even a few days—and it is okay if other people are disappointed, too. A healthy human is equipped to handle a wide range of emotions. We don't mature if we only experience the good ones. If you've ever raised a toddler, you know magic happens when he learns to associate bad choices with pain or unpleasantness. He learns something about the world when he experiences a negative emotion. We have a word for kids whose lives are designed so that they never hear no or experience disappointment: *spoiled.*

Yep, experiencing disappointment can actually help others grow. While it is our job to be kind, authentic, and caring, it is not our job to carry other people's feelings to the exclusion of our own. Everyone needs to be respectful of the feelings and opinions of others—but not ruled by them.

We have to let go of other's expecations for our lives. Freedom is on the other side of letting go. When others' opinions call all the shots, you are tied up and bound by their approval. And that's a really exhausting way to live. It may even mean you've lost the ability to listen to your gut; you may be totally unaware of what you even want.

Maybe you grew up in an environment where one or both

> When others' opinions call all the shots, you are tied up and bound by their approval.

of your parents expected you to meet their needs, not your own. Perhaps you have friendships with individuals who expect you to meet their needs but don't respect or support yours. Guess what? No more. No longer. Today you are going to embrace the fact that you can't control whether someone is disappointed by your no.

You can maintain these relationships, but the dynamic must shift if both parties are to move toward health and wholeness.

Truth 3: You Are the Only One Who Can Protect Your Boundaries

No one else can set appropriate boundaries for your life. It is your job to define where you stop and someone else begins.[8] Yes, I know. It would be so much easier if others just "got it," if they understood your perspective and respected your personhood without you having to be the bad guy who purposefully sets boundaries. Unfortunately, very few will help you set limits to promote and protect your mental health. It doesn't work that way. Takers will always take. It is your responsibility to set limits.

People who don't respect boundaries won't understand. All you can do is set them, enforce them, and let them deal with their feelings. This is not meant to sound harsh. I want you to see it as empowering. You don't have to be a victim to the demands of others. You can set limits on how much you'll do to keep another afloat or feeling good at your own expense.

Truth 4: Jesus, Not Your Yes, Determines Your Worth

When you say yes just to please another, you are letting pride control you. Pride says you must look good and can't risk falling out of favor by saying no. But, hear this bedrock truth: the only person who determines our worth is Jesus Christ, and he says we are precious and beloved just for being us—not for what we do or how we perform to the demands of another. His approval is

---

8   Henry Cloud and John Townsend, *Boundaries: When to Say Yes, When to Say No to Take Control of Your Life* (Grand Rapids: Zondervan, 1992).

what matters. Period. Not family, not friends, and certainly not strangers.

This is an exceptionally difficult truth for me, so know that I am in the trenches with you. *Every* day. I haven't perfected the art of no; I must still remind myself that I have worth apart from my yeses. I often remind myself that we are created to be people-*lovers*, not people-*pleasers*. It is our responsibility to love others without letting their behaviors or opinions devour our self-worth or dictate our choices.

Truth 5: Loving and Pleasing Are Separate

You may have lived your entire life believing that the Sunday school answer is to say yes and be polite, but remember, loving and pleasing are separate. While it is important to help and serve others when they are walking through difficult times—when they face loss, destruction, grief, illness, trauma, and loneliness—we are not called to please their whims. As believers, we are to be compassionate and caring to those who need help, but it is not caring to give endlessly and at the expense of our own health and well-being.

We must own our health and our boundaries. No one else is responsible for this hard work. In fact, it is in carrying our own load that we reach a place of wellness that enables us to help others. Choosing the right nos will leave us refreshed and ready when a friend is hurting and it's time to provide a yes.

Really, God is the ultimate model of healthy boundaries. He gives us the *choice* to choose him or deny him. His love is freely given, but he does not demand that we follow him or obey what he says. He lets us suffer the natural consequences of a life apart from him. He also deals with the sting of rejection that comes from those who don't choose him.

Matthew 5:37 says, "Let what you say be simply 'Yes' or 'No'; anything more than this comes from evil." Every time we say yes to something, we are saying no to something else, so pause and consider each answer. Our responses to others should never be determined by guilt, shame, or fear.

What are you saying no to because your yes has taken over? Is it time to rethink your boundaries as you learn to value self-care and authenticity?

Do This Instead: Work Towards Safety
1. Make Your Boundaries Clear

Boundaries define our space and who we are. It is our job to communicate what does and doesn't work for us. If our boundaries aren't clear, we can't expect people to respect them. Unexpressed expectations inevitably lead to resentment, so lay out your expectations in a way others can understand. Let others know the consequence of violating your established boundary. (See the exercise "Setting Boundaries" in the appendix). Remember, the consequence is always a change in *your* behavior or reaction. Consequences can never be about what the other will or won't do. You can't make someone stop yelling at you, but you can choose not to engage in a conversation if they are yelling.

Those who learn to use wisdom in opening and closing their drawbridge must also remember to hang a sign across the mote. This proclamation lets visitors know the rules of the castle. Without a sign, visitors must guess what is accepted inside the castle. They don't have a chance of getting it right. How do we expect others to respect our needs and boundaries when we are bashful about hanging out a sign?

Think of all the places that post signs and clearly articulate policy to help us understand what is expected—the "boundaries" of an environment or entity, if you will: Uber terms and agreements, school rules, hotel policy, emergency room procedure, college entrance requirements, and airline boarding protocol, to name a few. When we know what is expected, we are able to honor the expectations of organizations, environments, or even friends. Things run smoothly when everyone is clear, up-front, about what will be welcome and what will not be tolerated.

Work with me here. How many times have you experienced the downside of unspoken, unclear boundaries? Have you ever upset someone without knowing what you did because she wouldn't tell you? The confusion and angst is a product of unclear boundaries. She didn't post a sign outside of her castle. She didn't let you know what was okay, so you never had a chance to follow the rules or respect her space.

Think of all of the people who have an expectation of you. Nine times out of ten, they never articulate the expectation; thus, you are caught unaware when they become upset with you for not meeting the expectation. It's uncomfortable and awkward, and too many relationships have suffered all because we are afraid to be clear in advance about what we want and need.

Listen. If you want to get unstuck and enjoy your best life, it is your job to make sure your sign is clear and well communicated. You can't expect people to adhere to your boundaries if they don't know what they are.

I can think of a million different rules and ways to communicate them, and expectations might even change as new issues arise.

Rules for my castle (our house) might look like this. In this house we:

Rules for My Castle (Our House)

- Love God and love others
- Encourage each other
- Speak truth in love
- Ask for help
- Accept mistakes and learm from failure
- Celebrate each other's successes
- Don't have to hustle for our worth
- Know that we matter
- Know that we belong
- Clean up our belongings
- Make our beds
- Do our chores
- Lean in to uncomfortable conversations to understand each other
- Turn off technology at ___(assigned time)
- Serve others
- Speak with good purpose

Rules with friends:

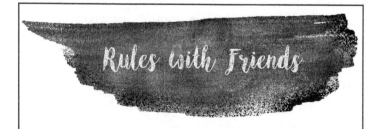

Rules with Friends

- We show up in authenticity
- We assume the best in each otheer
- We speak up in love if we are hurt
- We clarify miscommunication
- We don't expect our friends to meet our every need, or fix past hurts
- We love each other for who God designed them to be

2. Enforce Your Boundaries

Once you set your boundaries, it is your job to enforce them. If you don't enforce them as you said you would, you are giving away your power. We've all heard the parents of a toddler tell little Johnny to obey. When little Johnny doesn't, they say, "Don't make me count to five! One, two, three, three and a half, three and three quarters . . ." Johnny is only a toddler, but even *he* knows the consequence won't be enforced. The boundary isn't real if it's not enforced.

It requires fortitude to implement and practice the boundaries you set *before* the difficult interaction began. Everything seems so obvious when we think through our boundaries in a moment of quiet reflection, but let's face it, when enforcing boundaries with real people in hard situations, we don't want to be the bad guy. We don't want to offend someone. And we may still struggle to believe boundaries aren't rude and hurtful.

The truth is, if our boundaries are a challenge for someone else, it is *her* problem to deal with. We cannot set a boundary that will ensure our mental health and manage or regulate someone else's feelings at the same time. Putting ourselves in charge of keeping someone else feeling good is called codependency. And, let me be clear, codependency will wreck your mental well-being *every time.*

Rather, we need to let others manage their feelings. If we have set our boundaries in love—love is a crucial part of this equation—then we can rest, knowing we have done our part. We have explained what we will and will not do. We have established what we need in the relationship to keep ourselves healthy and headed in the right direction.

Their feelings over our boundary are not ours to own, fix, manage or change.

Their feelings over our boundary are not ours to own, fix, manage or change. We have to let people be responsible for their own feelings, and we have to let people learn from the disappointment they may feel when we enforce a boundary.

God calls us to love him and love others. He does not call us to be held hostage to other people's feelings. That is not love. It is bondage. As Brené Brown told *Oprah* magazine, "Daring to set boundaries is about having the courage to love ourselves even when we risk disappointing others."[9]

When you enforce your boundaries with people who have not been respecting you, they're not going to like it. If someone has become accustomed to controlling you or counting on you to bail her out, then, no, she is not going to want you to get healthy. It could look like a temper tantrum. It could look like passive-aggressive stonewalling. It could look like bullying or threatening. Remember, if you have lacked boundaries and left your drawbridge wide open in all previous interactions, then you are changing the game. People who don't respect other people's boundaries do not want the game changed. They want to be in control.

Remember, you have the power to grant or deny access to your soul space, just as you can open and close a drawbridge. You get to decide when to lower the drawbridge or raise it. When people are not respecting the rules on your sign, you need to ask them to leave. Ideally, they will choose to adjust and follow the rules so they can come back in.

Unfortunately, as others change and adapt to the new rules, things may get harder before they get easier. Allow time for individuals who need to regroup before they are willing to accept

---

9   http://www.oprah.com/spirit/how-to-set-boundaries-brene-browns-advice

your boundaries. Part of your respect toward their boundaries is providing time and space for them to adjust.

3. Show up in Love

When your boundaries are protected, you are free to show love. You are free to be present with the other, unfettered by misunderstanding and irritation. You are able to be kind because you are not inwardly seething with resentment as the other takes advantage of you again. You are not held captive by their aggressive or manipulative behavior. You have given the other a choice to be in a healthy relationship with you, and when he chooses to relate in a way that is good for all, you are free to shower him with love and compassion.

This is the kind of love Christ shows us. He waits for us to accept a right relationship with him. And when we do, we realize how much better life is when we are living according to the rules he has posted in his Word. So, when you are standing behind the sign you've posted, know that you are setting the other up to enjoy a better relationship. You are inviting her to mutual love and respect. It could look like this:

> "Hi, Aunt Sarah! I love having you come to visit. Unfortunately, we have decided that (we don't want cigarette smoke in our house), and when you (smoke in our house when you visit), it doesn't align with what works for us. If you are willing to (step into the backyard and smoke), then we would love to have you join us."
>
> Aunt Sarah: "Who do you think you are? How rude of you! I can't believe you won't just let me be who I am."

"Yep, I totally get that it doesn't make sense to you, but we've put some thought into this and hope that you'll consider our perspective. We would love to have you over again when you are willing to smoke outside."

Aunt Sarah: "Fine. Goodbye."

The beautiful thing is, you are now free to love Aunt Sarah without resentment or judgment because you have been honest and up-front about what you need. You won't feel bitter when she unknowingly violates what works for you. You are free to support her whether she chooses to respect your boundaries or not because you have been honest, and the choice is now up to her. If she chooses to stay away, that is her decision. How she feels about your boundary is none of your business.

> How she feels about your boundary is none of your business.

Reflection Questions:

1. With whom do you need more effective boundaries (family, friends, work, community, church, social media)? Why?

2. What has been the cost of not having clear boundaries in the areas above?

3. How can you stand firm and set necessary boundaries?

New Insight:
_____

_____
_____
_____
_____
_____
_____
_____
_____
_____
_____
_____
_____

Myth 7

I Can Do It All on My Own

We don't have to do all of it alone. We were never meant to.
—BRENÉ BROWN, *RISING STRONG*

So often, we don't want to ask for help. Why is that? Do we think it will make us weak or a burden? Will it signal that everyone else has it all together but we don't?

Instead of asking for assistance, we keep the struggle to ourselves, stuff our feelings, and push harder. We walk through life burdened while others offer help. At some point, we bought the lie that we deserve our burdens—and deserve to carry them alone.

My husband was deployed on the USS Ronald Reagan (CVN-76) when our daughter was two and our son was a newborn. We were fortunate that he was able to fly home for Luke's birth, but he had to leave two days later. I had a scheduled C-section, and while everything appeared to be normal, Luke was rushed to the NICU after his birth because he wasn't breathing on his own when he came out. I knew something was wrong the minute he was born because he wasn't crying. As a mother, that silence still haunts me.

Dave was back on the ship, Luke was in the NICU, I was trying to recover from a C-section and be at the hospital with Luke, and Keilah was a precocious two-year-old—precocious with a capital *P*. I was extremely lucky to have an amazing family who was a wonderful support system. I couldn't have done it without them. But it was very difficult for me to rely on them. I felt guilty that they stopped their lives to help with mine. I didn't want to let them help bear my burdens.

Fast-forward a year, and I was still drowning. Keilah was still precocious. Luke was still a baby, and Dave was still deployed off and on. I decided to look for a counselor, someone I could talk with to gain perspective and process my emotions.

Working with a counselor was new for me and, in all honesty, a little scary. I wasn't sure what to expect. (This was before I went back to school for a degree in counseling.) It ended up being the best investment I could have made. She called me out, gently, on the fact that I was trying to do it all alone—and no one is meant to do life alone.

Laura's Story: Unpacking Others' Baggage

Laura was a married forty-five-year-old with three grown children. She came to counseling wondering if she might have anxiety. Laura was not able to sleep well at night, was having occasional pain in her chest, and found it difficult to focus during the day due to repetitive thoughts and worries.

She had grown up as one of five siblings—the only girl and the youngest. Laura's dad died in a car accident when she was ten; a brother overdosed and died when she was twenty-five. Two brothers lived far away and didn't keep in touch. However, one lived near her, and she was closest to him. He was going through a messy divorce and needed help raising his nine-year-old son.

He had asked Laura if he and his son could move in with her temporarily, until he got back on his feet.

Her mother never remarried, and as the only daughter, Laura felt responsible to care for her. Laura's mom moved in with her family fifteen years ago, much to her family's disappointment. Her mom was difficult to have around, and Laura's husband and three children made it clear that she was a burden. Not wanting to hurt her mother, Laura felt like she didn't have a choice. Unfortunately, Laura's mom was demanding and shaming. She made it clear that she expected Laura to care for her every need.

Added to this significant family-of-origin pressure, Laura's marriage was struggling as well. Her husband had recently lost his job as a pharmaceutical salesperson due to company downsizing. He was a loyal, hardworking employee, and the layoff came as a complete surprise. Although he was actively looking for a job, Laura was carrying the financial burdens of the family. Her job as a nurse was consistent pay, but she was having to work overtime to pay the bills and make ends meet.

Laura also worried about her three teenage/young adult children. All three boys seemed to be doing well in life, but she was concerned about their future. Her oldest had just left for college, and she was worrying about his study habits. The other two were in high school and just getting by. Their grades were dropping, and one had been arrested for possession of marijuana.

What finally pushed Laura to seek counseling was the anxiety she was feeling. Really, anxiety? I can't figure out why (intended sarcasm). I was feeling anxious just listening to her. Laura was carrying everyone's burden, believing she had to figure it all out alone.

Truth 1: Asking for Help Is a Sign of Strength

Do you have a friend or family member who always seems to be taking, never giving back? You begin helping him with joy, happy you can help carry his burden. And then you help again. And again. Until you realize that while you are carrying his burdens, he is not carrying his own load (Galatians 6). Friends, we are called to carry one another's burdens, but we are called to carry our *own* loads.

I believe we have all been burned one way or another by taker-people, and because of how they operate, we are often afraid to be lumped into the "taker category." The last thing we want, as responsible people, is to be seen as takers. No. Thank. You.

But guess what? You aren't a taker. I know it's not you because you are doing the work to get unstuck and move forward. If you were content to live an unexamined, opportunistic life, you wouldn't be reading this book. In contrast, you are responsible, courageous, and willing to do the work. You just need permission to ask others to walk alongside you through the storms. You need to know that asking for help is not weakness. It is a sign of strength. It is an indication that you take

> You are winning when you have the courage to admit you can't do it alone.

your well-being seriously and are wise enough to know when a burden is too heavy to carry alone.

When storms come, you are brave in asking loved ones to support you. You are winning when you have the courage to admit you can't do it alone.

Truth 2: We Are Created for Community

We are created for connection, and connection comes through community. God made us this way because survival in groups is more certain than surviving as lone wanderers. Though we are no longer hunter-gatherer tribes organized for physical survival, we still need one another to be healthy and whole. A particular sense of well-being comes through connection that you simply cannot manufacture on your own. If you don't have a community of friends and family you can count on, it is time to find one. Book clubs, church groups, running clubs, dinner clubs, play dates with your kids, or professional groups are all good places to start. It may take time to find others to walk with, lean on, and care for; even so, connection is such a crucial part of being human you won't regret making the effort to find your modern-day tribe. After all, it's impossible to ask for help if you don't have close others to ask.

Do This Instead: Work Towards Unconditional Love
1. Show up and Be Present (In Person)

The trickiest thing about community is that you have to leave your house—and maybe your comfort zone—to find it. When we take a risk and show up, we gain community. We gain people who know us, see us, and want to support us. Though it may seem awkward at first, showing up is essential.

It is easy to hide in today's world. We can do virtually everything online. We can have groceries and meals delivered. Really, we can have almost anything delivered via Amazon Prime. We can watch church sermons online, and many of us work from home. So, getting out there takes effort. Even so, you are responsible for your life, and if you want to live it to the full, community must play a role. You can't be seen if you don't show up.

2. Be Vulnerable

No one can read your mind, and, certainly, no one will pry into your personal business. It is our responsibility to let others know where we need help—and that requires vulnerability.

As Brené Brown writes in *Rising Strong*, "Vulnerability is not winning or losing; it's have the courage to show up and be seen when we have no control over the outcome."[10] That's the hard part, right? It may feel scary having no control over how others will receive our admission that we are only human and sometimes need to lean on others. Control keeps us safe. It keeps us protected behind walls of superiority and confidence. And it keeps us alone. To create authentic connections with others, we must be vulnerable, allowing them to see our whole self—flaws and weaknesses included. The other option, as C. S. Lewis so eloquently describes in *The Four Loves*, is a life of darkness:

> To love at all is to be vulnerable. Love anything
> and your heart will be wrung and possibly
> broken. If you want to make sure of keeping it
> intact you must give it to no one, not even an
> animal. Wrap it carefully round with hobbies
> and little luxuries; avoid all entanglements.
> Lock it up safe in the casket or coffin of your
> selfishness. But in that casket, safe, dark,
> motionless, airless, it will change. It will
> not be broken; it will become unbreakable,
> impenetrable, irredeemable. To love is to be
> vulnerable.[11]

---

10   Brené Brown, *Rising Strong*, first edition (New York: Spiegel & Grau, an imprint of Random House, 2015).

11   C. S. Lewis, *The Four Loves* (New York: Harcourt, 1960).

Reflection Questions:

1. In what ways do you self-protect, avoid vulnerability, and stay isolated?
2. What keeps you from showing up as your authentic self or asking for the help you need?
3. Where could you create community or enter more fully into existing community?

New Insight:

_____

_____

_____

_____

_____

_____

_____

_____

_____

_____

_____

Myth 8

Busyness Helps Me Reach My Goals

If we don't know where we are going, any road will get you there.
–LEWIS CARROLL

You're busy. I get it. So am I. In a world where technology is supposed to save us time and create short cuts, the hustle seems more intense than ever. Oh, how I long to go back to days before cell phones and the internet. I think my brain would rest more. But . . . here we are, and technology is here to stay.

I have a question that might help with the hustle: are you working *harder* or *smarter*? Being busy doesn't mean you're productive. Constant striving doesn't guarantee you are going anywhere; it is possible to spin your wheels without accomplishing anything. What if our busyness is the very thing keeping us from reaching our goals?

Sometimes, we stay busy to avoid pain. We want to forget our feelings, and being busy helps us put problems on the back burner (until they boil over). The truth is, using busyness to numb our emotions will keep us running in circles, with no true resolution or progress. Often, the pain gets worse because we keep lumping other feelings of hurt or pain on top, instead of connecting the dots in our own story.

Sometimes, we are distracted by our to-do list, and distraction keeps us from seeing what we are truly meant to do. And checking things off of that list is instant therapy or gratification for those avoiding the bigger picture. We are playing small parts in accomplishing everyone else's goals while never showing up to star in our own feature film.

Ashley's Story: Busting Out of Busyness

Ashley was running and running. She never seemed to stop. Not only was she a self-diagnosed workaholic, working long hours, saying yes to everything, and taking on every team project thrown her way, but she also overextended herself with personal activities. She was in charge of her son's little league team, running the schedule and communicating with the parents on the coach's behalf. She was also the team mom for her daughter's dance team, and she volunteered to teach Sunday school at church with the three-year-old class.

As I was getting to know Ashley, I was confused. She came to see me because she felt overworked and exhausted. Yet, when I asked her what she could eliminate from her plate, she wasn't willing to let anything go. She was protective of her commitments and had a fierce determination to stay busy.

Ashley's frenzy became clearer when I searched below her surface complaint to access areas she clearly didn't want to discuss. Ashley's parents divorced when she was seven. Her mom told her that her dad was an alcoholic. She said she didn't remember much about her father, other than him yelling at her mom often. She had memories of him holding her too tight and scaring her and remembered feeling frightened for her mom and older brother, whom he beat on occasion.

She spent her childhood believing it was her job to protect her mom and to keep her mom from feeling alone or scared. She often missed social events with friends because she didn't want to leave her mom home alone. She took on a part-time job in high school, in addition to her rigorous coursework, because she wanted to help pay the bills.

Without realizing it, she became the parent in her father's stead. She tried to become the partner who could carry the burden of her mom's sadness. She was so busy making sure her mother was okay that she failed to recognize her own hurt and rejection. Her dad's absence affected her, too, but she stuffed the negative feelings deep down and kept them hidden beneath a cover of busyness. Managing her mom's emotions was a full-time job. Ashley had plenty to do to make sure her mom never again experienced pain like she did when her dad left.

As an adult, Ashley moved out of the house but stayed close by. Leaving for college wasn't an option because anything far away was out of the question. She went to a local community college for two years and then finished her degree online.

When she was twenty-five, Ashley fell in love with Kyle, a coworker from her accounting office. They married and began a family when she was twenty-seven. Ashley shared with Kyle that when they could afford a house with an extra bedroom, she planned on having her mom live with them so that they could take care of her as she got older. Kyle never questioned it, thinking it would be years before it actually happened. Except it wasn't. Ashley's mom moved in with them ten years into their marriage and planned on living with them indefinitely. Ashley couldn't figure out why Kyle seemed annoyed by her mom's constant presence and her own constant absence as she stayed at work long hours. She wished he understood her need to work hard to support her mom and their family.

Their homelife felt chaotic because they were constantly rushing to events. The kids had no structure and were struggling academically and socially. Due to Ashley's stress, she frequently erupted on all family members and her coworkers. She told me, "They just don't get it." She felt no one understood how hard she was working and how much she was juggling.

Have you noticed a pattern in Ashley's life? She was numbing her pain by keeping busy, and the busyness was focused on the wrong things.

Truth 1: Busyness Numbs Pain (But Only Temporarily)

Ashley was doing anything she could to avoid pain. She had unaddressed childhood trauma, losing her father and taking on the responsibility of being a partner and coparent with her mom. To handle the pressure and pain, she adopted busyness as a coping strategy. The problem is, ignoring her story doesn't heal it. It only makes it bigger and deeper until the pressure causes her to lash out at someone else. We can't heal from our story unless we do the work to walk through it. Distractions only keep us trapped. The pain will come out eventually, often in a behavior or addiction. Though busyness might seem harmless, even praiseworthy in American society, it can become an addiction when we use it to block emotion and vulnerability.

> Though busyness might seem harmless, even praiseworthy in American society, it can become an addiction when we use it to block emotion and vulnerability.

Imagine someone attacks you with a knife. Imagine the pain you feel from the deep wound he inflicts. Now, imagine you ignore the wound instead of giving it the attention it deserves. You just look the other way and pretend the streaming blood is no big deal. What would happen? You might feel faint from a loss of blood or stain your surroundings red. Left untreated, the gash would eventually get infected and ooze green pus. Yep, that's an unpleasant visual. I know. Sorry. But, here's the thing: our untreated emotional wounds can be just as unappealing. Those around us can see the ooze. They are left to deal with the blood stains we've left behind.

Staying busy seems effective—in the short-term—at keeping the pain from consuming us. However, over time, the charade eats up all our energy and keeps us from focusing on the things that actually matter.

Truth 2: Busyness Blocks Purpose

When avoiding pain drives our day, we spend our time running from the past instead of running toward future goals. We miss out on becoming who we are created to be as we try to forget who we were in an earlier, more painful stage. When we deny part of our story, it's as if we have a big hole in our identity. We are incomplete and afraid, constantly managing the fear of what might happen if we let ourselves slow down and feel. It's very difficult to serve, love, or be close to another if we are stuck in survival mode, just doing, doing, doing, never feeling.

It's very difficult to serve, love, or be close to another if we are stuck in survival mode, just doing, doing, doing, never feeling.

Humans are equipped for survival with three responses to stress: fight, flight, and freeze. Addiction to busyness is like being stuck in flight mode all day, every day. You will never find peace or belonging or purpose when you are in flight mode. Flight is meant to be a temporary reaction, a proper response to danger that will keep you moving until you get to safety. If you have allowed flight mode—which might look like a busy frenzy to prove your worth—to control years or decades of your life, it's time to slow down. You are created for more. You deserve to live your life with passion and purpose.

Do This Instead: Work Towards Validation
1. Examine Your Passions

If you could stop running and stop spinning your wheels, what would you do with your time instead? What are your core values, the things that make you want to speak up and make a difference? What are your hopes and dreams, the plans you made when you were a young woman and didn't allow perceived limitations to control you? Your answers determine where your focus should be.

Positive psychology uses the word *flow* to describe what happens when you are working within your purpose and passion. You enter a "zone" where time flies and the rest of the world recedes as you are consumed with the task at hand. The task so closely aligns with your interests and abilities that it is not a chore or mere busyness; it is touching a deep part of your identity and purpose.

Maya Angelou is quoted as saying, "My mission in life is not merely to survive, but to thrive; and to do so with some passion, some compassion, some humor, and some style." Ladies! You were not just created to survive. You heard Maya; we need to thrive! Thriving looks different for everyone. Your version of thriving will look very different than my version of thriving, but it will never look like

> Your version of thriving will look very different than my version of thriving, but it will never look like desperate overcommittment and stress.

desperate overcommittment and stress. Figure out your passions so that you know where you need to concentrate your activity.

2. Examine Your Strengths

Busyness doesn't matter if we are investing in areas that don't suit us. Do you know your strengths? If not, may I recommend a few personality assessments? You'll find many resources online, but here are a few to consider as you begin this journey: the Strengthsfinder 2.0;[12] the Enneagram[13]; the Myers-Briggs Type Indicator (adapted in *Please Understand Me*) [14]; or the DiSC profile, which can be taken online. Identifying the way you are wired is the first step to knowing where to invest your time.

> Identifying the way you are wired is the first step to knowing where to invest your time.

Knowing your personality type will help you understand the types of activities that will feel effortless and natural. For instance, if you are an introvert but spend your time around people all day, you may come home exhausted. If you enjoy leading and hate feeling controlled, you may wither away in a cubicle but find exhilaration from starting your own company. Live in your sweet spot and outsource the rest. Delegate. Say no to anything that doesn't align with your skills and interests. The world needs *your* skills and gifts.

---

12   Tom Rath, *Strengthsfinder 2.0* (New York: Gallup Press, 2007).
13   Ian Morgan Cron and Suzanne Stabile, *The Road Back to You: An Enneagram Journey to Self-Discovery* (Downers Grove, IL: InterVarsity Press, 2016).
14   David Keirsey and Marilyn Bates, *Please Understand Me: Character and Temperament Types* (Del Mar, CA: Prometheus Nemesis Book Company, 1984).

In *Strengthsfinder 2.0,* Tom Rath references *Rudy*, a 1993 film that depicts the true story of a young man named Daniel "Rudy" Ruettiger who had a passionate dream to play football for Notre Dame. The problem, however, was that Rudy wasn't qualified academically or physically to be admitted to Notre Dame or to make the football team. That didn't stop Rudy; he had determination like no other. He jumped through hoops and overcame obstacles to make his way into the school and onto the team. He never got to play, though, until the final game of his senior year. The coach, responding to pressure from Rudy's teammates and the fans who knew his story, finally sent him on the field. Not only was the whole stadium chanting, "Rudy, Rudy," but his teammates even carried him off of the field at the end. It is a beautiful, inspirational story. Or is it?

Without a doubt, Rudy has amazing grit and determination. But, what if he had used that grit and determination toward his skill sets? He was busy alright, but busy focusing on something that he was not created for (college football). Imagine if he was busy working within his sweet spot. Imagine the business he could have built or the problems he could have solved if he was working within his strengths.

3. Examine Your Obstacles and Make Space

What is getting in the way of reaching your potential and fulfilling your purpose? Identify the empty tasks or defeating mind-sets that hijack your forward motion. Even the "good" can hinder you from reaching the "great." Think through your day. Which activities are merely a good way to pass the time? Which are aligned with your ultimate goals and growth? What could you hire out or have delivered to buy time for more important pursuits? Look for a cleaning service, order groceries online, pay someone to walk your dog. The list will be unique to you, but each of us can learn to optimize our use of time. Take a moment and use the "Life Balance Wheel" I've provided in the appendix to assess areas of your life keeping you from focusing on what is most important.

Or maybe *you* are your biggest obstacle. What negative thoughts intervene when you start to imagine what could be? Are you quick to predict failure? Do you jump to negative conclusions when you consider a risk you want to take or a new venture you feel led to? Have you labeled yourself as stupid or incompetent? You must eliminate these thoughts. Think of a positive opposite thought and make it your new mantra. How can you eliminate the obstacle of limited thinking?

Once you know what you really want, you can identify where your strengths and talents lie and then eliminate, outsource, or delegate anything that doesn't align with your passions and strengths.

Being busy doesn't mean you are accomplishing anything. In fact, most of the time, busyness hinders you from reaching your goals. Work smarter, not just harder, and cultivate your unique strengths.

Reflection Questions:

1. In what ways do you use busyness to hide the real work you are called to do?
2. Where should you invest your time instead?
3. How are you uniquely wired? In what situations do you shine?
4. What slows you down or keeps you from reflecting on and pursuing your life's true purpose?

New Insight:
_____

_____
_____
_____
_____
_____
_____
_____
_____
_____
_____
_____

I Must Tolerate Toxic People

I can go back there like it is yesterday. Junior high. Bad bangs, bushy eyebrows, blue eye shadow, crimped hair, fluorescent T-shirts, and all. If you weren't raised in the '80s, you missed out on some totally rad fashion styles.

Along with fluorescent shirts and parachute pants, I also remember the girl drama of my teenage years: the queen bees, the criticism, the hurt feelings, and the exclusion. Junior high was one of the most difficult stages in my life, and I imagine it was in yours, too. I remember friends I didn't feel safe with, parties I felt uncomfortable at, and boys I felt weird talking to. Everyone else seemed so comfortable around each other. Why did it seem like I was the only one who didn't know how to talk to people? "I would love to go back and relive my junior high years because they were so great," said no human ever.

In fact, when I am working with clients, much of the trauma work we do originates from those early teen years. Body changes, hormones, and friend dynamics are just some of the memories that show up. And all this flux and change is even more troubling if the individual was also dealing with family struggles or lacked a safe adult to guide her through the tumultuous season.

One thing is certain about adolescence: we get our first taste of relational drama. Sadly, some teens deal with social pressure and uncertainty by becoming hateful and aggressive, cannibalizing the self-worth of "friends" and classmates. In other words, junior high breeds toxic people. With less parental oversight and jarringly strong hormones, kids run amuck and develop some pretty harmful interpersonal patterns. Sadly, some never learn a new pattern and continue to use, manipulate, and betray those closest to them.

While some of us are lucky enough to get a taste of the drama, realize how damaging it is, and instead move toward healthier relationships, others end up on the drama train for life. Some of us are running the drama on the train. Many don't want the drama but don't know how to get off of the train, unsure of how to disengage without seeming heartless. We may fear what the other will do. We may question whether the drama is really that big of a deal, and it is. Drama and relational turmoil can keep you stuck and will often distract you from your goals and plans. What would it look like to say no to toxic people?

Megan's Story: From Weighted Down to Lifted Up

Megan was a forty-year-old mother of two. She came to me completely depleted, trying to please everyone in her life except herself.

As I got to know Megan, she gave me a brief description of her upbringing. She described a dad who was passive and withdrawn and a mother she could never please. Her grades were never high enough. She was never thin enough. She was never pretty enough.

Feeling like love was nonexistent from her dad and conditional from her mom, she turned to friends to be her support network. The problem is, her friends were not safe either. Even though they were toxic, she clung to her group of friends as she was desperate for love, acceptance, and affirmation. (Aren't we all?)

Megan recalled times during high school when she just wanted to be noticed. She hung out with a certain group of girls, even though they were mean. She wanted to fit in and was glad to be somewhat included, reasoning it was better to be on the fringe of a mean group than to have no friends at all.

High school was filled with constant highs and lows for Megan. Friends were mean to her one day and then friendly the next. She couldn't help but feel used at times; her group would ask to hang out at her spacious house by her pool and then practically ignore her while they were there. They would talk about times they got together without her and how much fun they had, as if she were invisible. Megan teared up at the memory.

When Megan arrived at college, she was excited to start fresh with a new environment and new friends. Quickly, though, Megan found herself back in the same situation. She was drawn to new friends on her dorm floor, immediately feeling grateful to have met some girls, but as time went on, she noticed the same patterns. These girls would also alternately leave her out and then include her. She felt disposable, as if they didn't really care whether she was around. However, just as she was beginning to make other friends, they would pull her back in. For Megan, just like in high school, the cost of being excluded sometimes was worth the high she got when she was invited.

When I saw Megan, she had just moved from the city to the suburbs and was getting to know her new neighbors. While she was happy in her job, her marriage, and her parenting, finding friends was, again, fraught with pain.

The first woman she met on her street was super friendly. Her name was Chelsea, and they immediately connected. Megan was grateful that Chelsea lived so close and was happy to be included with a few other friends for book club. She felt a little uncomfortable when Chelsea would speak negatively about the other women in the neighborhood who weren't there, but Megan thought that maybe she was just being too sensitive.

Time went on, and she and Chelsea became close friends. Megan's husband, Rob, noticed how happy his wife was. Megan felt like she finally belonged—until Chelsea had a birthday dinner party at a local restaurant and didn't invite Megan. And then posted about it all over social media. Ouch. When Megan got the courage to ask about the party, Chelsea dismissed her hurt, explaining there weren't enough spots at the restaurant, though she wished she could have included her. Chelsea couldn't figure out why she was so hurt; she acted as if Megan's sensitivity was the problem.

As time went on, it became clear that Chelsea was the neighborhood queen bee. She ran the show. She decided who could be friends with whom, and she used invitations to events to maintain control and power. She immediately befriended anyone new in the neighborhood to keep everyone where she wanted them—in her inner or outer circle. The problem was, neighbors in the circle never knew if they were in or out. It was hard to predict. Chelsea was friendly and wonderful one day, and then, without notice, she would cause others to wonder what they did to upset her. Chelsea was like a magnet who drew people toward her. She was outgoing, fun, and personable, and made everyone around her feel like they mattered. She led the women in the neighborhood to believe that she truly desired a friendship, only to betray them when the mood struck her.

Megan carried the hurt and pain of feeling excluded as if it were a fifty-pound weight. It seemed like she was right back in middle school. The same feelings arose in her, and she had to keep reminding herself that she was a forty-year-old woman. She asked herself, "Why do I let this woman get to me? Why is being left out such a big deal to me?"

It is a big deal. Being left out hurts. Whether you are in kindergarten and the girls on the playground won't let you play house or eighty-five years old and excluded from Bingo night at the retirement home, we all need to be seen, known, and loved. We long to know we matter.

The truth is, we are seen, known, and loved by our Father in heaven. Even so, we are wired to connect and were created to be seen, known, and loved by friends and family here on earth. When those connections go wrong, it produces hurt. With wisdom, we learn from painful interactions and identify the people who are creating all the drama—and then we steer clear.

Truth 1: You Can Identify What Toxic Means to You

Friends, plain and simple, toxic people keep us stuck. How do you know if you have a toxic person in your life? First and foremost, you can tell because of the hurt you constantly feel when you are around her. Train yourself to notice when others:

Toxic People

- Put you down
- Are draining
- Are boundary-less
- Guilt you into meeting their needs and expectations
- Are fake with you
- Spread negativity
- Gossip about others
- Judge
- Don't apologize
- Criticize
- Monopolize your time
- Tell you who you can and can't be friends with
- Are jealous
- Are envious

- Don't care about you
- Are self-absorbed
- Won't take responsibility for thier actions
- Act as if nothing is ever enough
- Feel threatened by your other relationships
- Set impossible expectations
- Are controlling
- Are inconsistent
- Don't respect "no"
- Lie to you
- Only speak and never listen
- Are easily angered
- Isolate you

Be aware of these signs and also pay attention to the visceral cues your body gives you. Do you cringe when you think about being around a certain person? Is there an uneasy feeling in your stomach? Do words catch in your throat? Do you feel depleted, worthless, less-than, frustrated, or sad from your time with her? You may wish she could see how

> Friends, if being around a toxic person costs you your peace, the cost is too high.

hurtful her behavior is, but when you try to explain how it impacts you, she just dismisses it.

Friends, if being around a toxic person costs you your peace, the cost is too high. You have a choice. You can decide when a "friendship" isn't worth the drama. You can walk away. In time, you will find healthier friends. You will. It just takes strength and determination to try something new.

Truth 2: You Won't Change the Toxic Person

I have been that person, and I am guessing you have been that person, too. We think, *If I can just help her see how her behavior impacts others, she'll change.*

Yep. You can relate, can't you? Most of us stay in toxic relationships too long, especially those of us who are prone to saving others. We want to fix her and repair the relationship, hoping to make it stronger. But change would take remorse and humility on the part of the toxic person, and, sadly, that is just not going to happen. Toxic people won't apologize. They won't look at the harm they are inflicting or change their patterns of manipulation and control. They are not able to self-reflect.

Now, let me be clear. No one is past help. Everyone can change. But it will require deep, deep work on the part of the unhealthy person. You cannot save someone else or tell them it is time to be different. We can only work on ourselves. So, check your motivation. Why are you staying in this toxic relationship? What insecurities are keeping you from walking away? What do you get from that person that keeps you entangled and controlled?

Sometimes we cannot avoid the toxic people in our life. It might be an immediate family member, a relative, a neighbor, or a coworker. In those cases, it is essential to set clear boundaries and establish what you are willing to tolerate and what does not work for you. If clear boundaries are not working, it might be time to cut off ties. Ask the Holy Spirit for wisdom and discernment when you must stay in a relationship. You do not have to compromise your mental well-being, so carefully consider what is yours to do in each relationship. Have the courage to love yourself enough to set limits with those who are not healthy for you. Your self-care must come first.

> We must develop healthy relationships and find friends who fill us up, make us better, and cheer us on.

Truth 3: Safe People Are Everywhere

Often, we miss the safe people already in our life because we can't see past the drama. Or the drama seems interesting, and the safe people feel boring. In our quest to get unstuck and be our best selves, we must develop healthy relationships and find friends who fill us up, make us better, and cheer us on. Safe people place no expectations on you; rather, they are:

Safe People

- Encouraging
- Supportive
- Happy for you when you succeed
- Not threatened by your other relationships
- Authentic
- Trustworthy
- Trusting
- Forgiving
- Predictable
- Consistent

Do This Instead: Work Towards Loving Relationships

1. Examine the Toxicity in Your Life

Who sucks the life out of you? Who keeps your stomach in knots? Conversely, who supports you and helps you grow? Who cheers you on and keeps no record of wrongs? These questions are important, so take a moment and think about those who surround you. Make a list. Put a plus sign by those who encourage, motivate, and energize you. Put a minus sign by those who leave you feeling drained, less than, or unhappy. You likely already know who the negative people are. You probably get nervous and feel tension in your body before or after you hang out with them. You may even turn to others for support in dealing with them. While they may never change, you have the option to change your response by pulling away or establishing boundaries.

> Life is too short to remain tethered to toxic people.

Who we spend our time with has an enormous impact on our happiness and our success. And, because of the quick tempo of life with career and family, we only have limited time for a small circle of friendships. Are those people building you up? Life is too short to remain tethered to toxic people.

2. Decline Invitations to Board the Drama Train

When drama shows up, respectfully say no. Toxic people won't be disappointed that you rejected them. They will be disappointed that they can't control you anymore. They will be sad that they don't have power over you.

In essence, you are choosing your own self-worth over their desire to control you. Don't buy the lie that it is selfish to consider your relational needs. We are called to love others, not be controlled by them. It is not our job to manage other people's happiness. They must make their own choices and also sit in the consequences of their decisions.

But be prepared. When you decline the invitation to ride the drama train, you will get rejected. Those who are on the train will scoff at you for not climbing aboard. They want you to validate their choice to ride. It's okay. You need to let go of the need to be all things to all people—especially the toxic ones. If you receive rejection through name calling, protesting, backstabbing, and social-media blasting, then celebrate. That means you did the right thing, as they are showing their true character.

I know. You are thinking, *Kim, that sounds easy on paper, but actually getting off the train will be impossible. These toxic people are family members, coworkers, or neighbors I can't get away from.* In those instances, you must flex your boundary muscles. You are stronger than you think. Remember, when we set boundaries, we don't do it with a grenade. We do it in love. We kindly explain what is okay for us and then we move to the side so that we do not receive their toxic reaction.

3. Find People Who Value You

Now that you are off the drama train, find your people. We've already talked about how crucial community is, but here I am telling you that finding the *right kind* of community is even more critical. Seek relationships with safe people who will support you, encourage you, and be happy for your successes. Safe people will value your happiness. They won't use or manipulate you to serve their ends. They won't rely on you to make them whole.

If you have been on the drama train for a while, it might take some time to find healthier friendships. That is okay. It is better to be alone than with toxic others. Once Megan was able to see Chelsea for who she was, she invested in different relationships.

She met other neighbors and sought women who would be safe friends. Other options are out there. It's not a dichotomous choice of toxic friend or no one. Just be patient and hold tight to what you know is best for you in the long run.

4. Know Yourself

The time you have after disengaging from toxic relationships can be a fruitful time to grow in self-knowledge. Use the empty space to clarify your values, your strengths, and your passions. Who do you want to invest time in? What qualities are important in a friend? What are your dreams? What will it take to get there? What is keeping you stuck? What kind of person will draw out your inner strengths?

Friends, hear me. You are enough. You do not need to prop yourself up with toxic people. I know it feels like a risk, and hard days may come after it's done, but it is okay to get off of the train. It will be worth it.

Reflection Questions:

1. Who makes you feel depleted, rather than recharged, after you spend time together? What recent social interactions have drained you? Why?
2. What's one step you can take today to get unstuck by saying no to toxic people?
3. Why have you resisted setting boundaries with toxic people? How can you create healthy boundaries moving forward?

New Insight:

I Am Not Ready

You don't have to see the whole staircase. Just take the first step.
—Martin Luther King Jr.

I can be the worst at putting things off. Truly. I know that sounds funny coming from someone who works as a coach and counselor and helps others *not* to put things off. Don't look in the gardener's garden.

As I reflect, it is not so much that I put things off but that I am afraid to jump in. I am afraid to really experience what God has planned for me. It seems so much easier to stay small and hide.

The truth is, I get overwhelmed with the things I know God has called me to do. They seem so big. I knew I was created to be a therapist. It has been in my heart from an early age. I love working with people. I love helping people. I love walking with others, assuring them it is going to be okay and letting them know that they don't have to do it alone.

Despite feeling called, in all honesty, I didn't think that I could do it. Going back to get my master's degree felt overwhelming. During that season, Dave was often deployed with the military, and I was raising two little ones. The time never seemed right, and even though I felt God had made it clear, the journey felt too long, too daunting. How could I do it? How could I juggle it all?

And now, I am in another season of growth and change. I have known for years that I needed to rise up and share more. God has, again, called me to impact others, to call out the lies we tell ourselves and empower women to be *all* we are created to be. But that feels scary, too. I am not sure how this journey will look. It's a new season. I've never written a book before! The entire writing process scared me when I looked at the mountain of work that goes into writing a book. How could I scale those heights?

Isn't this the way it must be with farmers? Each spring, they feel the possibility of planting and preparing. Their fields are fallow and waiting for new life. If the farmer got hung up on the storms that might come or the drought he might face, he'd never have the gumption to plant the first seed. If, on the first day of spring, he tried to summon all the strength he'd need for plowing and weeding and harvesting throughout the entire season, he'd feel absolutely defeated.

Like the farmer, we can talk ourselves out of taking the first step. We can look at the finish line and feel pressure to be ready right away for the entire trip. I love the verse in Isaiah that reminds us we don't have to have everything figured out before we begin. We can trust God to give us direction *as we need it*: "And I will lead the blind in a way that they do not know, in paths that they have not known I will guide them. I will turn the darkness before them into light, the rough places into level ground. These are the things I do, and I do not forsake them" (Is. 42:16). He will give us light along the way. We don't have to be ready today for what the journey might require in a year. What a relief!

So, what stops us? What limits what we expect from life or the risks we are willing to take? Why do we stay small instead of pursuing our audacious, God-given dreams?

Alexis's Story: Living Our Best Lives

Alexis was a thirty-year-old married female who taught third grade at a local elementary school and loved her job working with kids. She described the joy she felt when she saw her students' minds working and growing. While Alexis loved her students, she was not passionate about working in the classroom. She felt limited by the four walls and the time she was committed to be there. She was frustrated because she loved what she did but knew she wanted more.

Alexis and I spent time working on strengths and personality assessments to clarify her gifts. We determined that she had the desire to be in a leadership role but didn't have the confidence to step out.

I asked Alexis what she wanted. Hesitantly and reluctantly, she shared that she wanted to be a principal. "Great!" I said with great enthusiasm. "You will be a wonderful principal!" In addition, I learned the school system she worked for would actually pay for her master's degree. A total win!

Her reply surprised me: "Well . . . I am not sure I am going to pursue it."

I was confused. Why? Why in the world would she not pursue it? We had determined she was wired for a leadership role. We knew she loved being around and working with children. It was evident she had the ability to perform the role and had the time and resources to pursue an advanced degree.

After further exploration, I discovered that Alexis's parents were both teachers as well. They both had their undergraduate degrees and teaching credentials but did not have a higher education degree. Alexis shared memories of her dad's shame in being turned down when he attempted to become a principal during his years in education. He was told he wasn't the right person for the job. She observed his hurt for years and watched him stuff his pain into alcohol.

There it was. I saw it clearly. Alexis believed the lie that she needed to stay small to keep her parents from feeling ashamed that they had never moved higher. She was letting her dad's regrets paralyze her future. She was sacrificing her own life and happiness for her dad's.

Here's the truth: Alexis is not responsible for her dad's shame. It is not her job to make him feel better about his challenges. It is her job to make the world a better place. It is *my* job to make the world a better place. It is *your* job to make the world a better place. If we don't figure out what is holding us back from living our best lives, we are robbing others from our gifts.

> If we don't figure out what is holding us back from living our best lives, we are robbing others from our gifts.

Have you heard the story about the man who was on top of his house during a flood? The water was rising higher and higher as a rowboat approached him and offered him a ride.

"No, thank you," he said. "I believe that God is going to rescue me." So, the rowboat went on.

The water kept rising. This time, a man in a canoe came up to him, offering him escape. Again, the man said, "No, thank you. I believe God is going to rescue me." So, the canoe went on.

The water was almost to the top of the roof, and a rescue helicopter approached him, lowering the rope ladder. "No, thank you," said the man. "I believe that God is going to rescue me." So, the helicopter went on.

Unfortunately, the waters rose too high, and the man died. When he was face-to-face with God in heaven, he asked, "Lord, why didn't you save me? My faith was strong, but here I am, in heaven."

The Lord looked at him and said, "What do you mean? I sent you a boat, a canoe, and a helicopter. What else could I have done?"

Friends, we are created to do amazing things. We are created to shine. Look around. God is sending you invitations to do the work he has called you to and equipped you for. It is time to get in the boat.

Truth 1: The "Perfect Time" Does Not Exist

The illusion of "perfect timing" is a powerful component of the myth "I'm not ready." We have a dream but reason it's best to wait until we feel absolutely secure, safe, and ready—with all the unknowns worked out. However, waiting for the perfect time actually keeps us frozen in place. Circumstances will never be just right; schedules will never open up; and our commitments will not someday become hassle-free. Life is not going to slow down so you can get the perfect start. You just have to do it. Start where you are. Say no to procrastination and wasting time and say yes to the exciting passion you feel stirring in your heart. While we can't control our circumstances, we can choose the best option in the moment that will lead us to our goals.

If we don't create a plan, by default, someone else's plan will dominate our lives. But someone else's plan will not make your heart sing or fill you with purpose.

> If you really want to accomplish something, you will find a way. If you keep finding excuses, you will likely end up in regret.

The late Jim Rohn is quoted as saying, "We all must suffer one of two things: the pain of discipline, or the pain of regret." If you really want to accomplish something, you will find a way. If you keep finding excuses, you will likely end up in regret.

It may be helpful to spend time with a coach or counselor to clarify your unique gifts and how to use them in service of what you want. It is time to make *you* a priority. Of course, I am not suggesting you neglect your family, quit your job, or drop every commitment. I am saying take the first step in figuring it all out. What comes first? Prioritize the important things and let the other things go for a season. You can always binge watch *The Bachelor* once your project is complete. How amazing it will feel to have something to show for the time and talents you've been given.

Truth 2: Fear Keeps You Small

Humans feel fear. It has kept us alive as a species. Consider your ancestors. If there was no fear response, they wouldn't have run from the predator or protected their families from threat. So, fear can be beneficial, but it also has an underbelly.

When we let fear move beyond its legitimate purpose to protect and allow it to infect our perspective on situations that are not life and death, that's a problem. That brand of fear holds us back. It might make you label yourself: "I'm too _____ to ever be able to _____." It might make you think, "If I'm not 100 percent successful, I have failed." Fear will engage your mind in every negative outcome that could occur. It will convince you that stepping out and taking a chance is way too risky. Fear will keep you small.

I am begging you to talk back to fear. Thank it for protecting you when you are in a truly dangerous situation. And then politely ask it to go away and allow you to dream, to create, and to be you.

Revealing your passions to others can make you feel vulnerable—of course you'd like them to approve. But don't confuse vulnerability with danger. Don't let fear hold you back.

Do This Instead: Work Towards Wisdom

1. Change the What Ifs

When fear steps out of line, it can make you feel inferior. It tells you failure is the most likely scenario. I feel fear when I write or speak as fear makes me wonder, who would want to listen to me anyhow? Some call this impostor syndrome; fear can make you ask, "Who am I to share? Who am I to speak up?"

It can also look like this: What if they don't like what I write? What if I miscommunicate my message? What if I embarrass myself? The what-ifs seep in unconsciously and control our choices and our emotions.

What keeps me going to push through the discomfort is listening to *this* what-if instead: *What if I miss the opportunity to impact others because I didn't step out?* That is the what-if that keeps me going. Flip the script on the what-ifs and allow the fear of missing out to propel you forward.

> Flip the script on the what-ifs and allow the fear of missing out to propel you forward.

2. Create Specific Steps to Success

We often put things off because our goals seem too big. They seem too far away. Too unrealistic. We are thinking about the entire scope of the project instead of just one achievable action to get us on our way. You've likely heard this motivational question before: "How do you eat an elephant? One bite at a time." That concept applies here.

Instead of focusing on the enormity of the task, set goals that are manageable. While it is a well-known acronym, I am a huge fan of SMART goals.

Is your goal *specific*? Broad goals get us nowhere. Imagine my goal is to "be happy." Well, what does happy look like? There could be millions of definitions for this broad term. Happy for me is sitting in a French café in the spring, reading a great book and sitting next to my husband. Is that what happy looks like for you? Probably not. Goals need to identify who, when, where, what, and why.

Is your goal *measureable*? How do you know when you've reached the goal? Graduating college and getting a degree is a measurable goal. Starting a company is not a measurable goal, unless you add in specifics, like securing funding and setting up a website.

Is your goal *achievable*, something you are capable of reaching? Is it attainable? If I set the goal to become a professional football player, it would not be achievable. First of all, I would need to be a man; I would also need to be much larger than my 5' 3" frame.

Is your goal *relevant*? Does it align with your life, values, and mission? Is it something you believe needs to be done? Writing a book or doing a TED talk is a realistic goal for me. They both align perfectly with my desire to positively impact the world and to challenge women to live their best lives. Going back to school to become an astronaut does not align with my mission or values.

Is your goal *timed*? What will you do by when? We all need deadlines so that we know how to apportion our time. If we set goals without measuring when we will have it done, we might as well not set the goal. I would argue this is one area many fail in. They don't hold themselves accountable to a timed deadline. Don't skip this step. Create your own SMART goals with the exercise I provide in the appendix.

Step out. Face the fear. Don't panic that you aren't ready. Stare anxiety in the face and press on.

You are courageous. Don't let procrastination or doubt get in the

Be seen. Be known. Be loved.

way of what you are called to do. Do something your future self will thank you for. Be seen. Be known. Be loved.

Reflection Questions:

1. In what ways does fear keep you from living a life aligned with your purpose and passions?
2. How can you bolster your confidence and take a step toward your SMART goal(s) *now*?
3. What types of excuses show up repeatedly in your life?

New Insight:

_____

_____

_____

_____

_____

_____

_____

_____

_____

_____

_____

_____

Being Popular Is More Valuable Than Being Yourself

I'm sorry that people are so jealous of me.
But I can't help that I'm popular.
–Gretchen Wieners, *Mean Girls*

I saw Taylor Swift on her Red tour with my daughter. Keilah was thirteen at the time, and she looked up to Taylor with childlike admiration. Not only did she love her music, but she also loved Taylor's authenticity and apparent desire to be a role model for young girls.

As Taylor was leading into a song, she said something to the girls in the audience: "Girls, you know how adults tell us as kids that when we grow up, people will stop being mean? I believed them. But, that's not true. People are still mean." She went on to challenge the girls to find the right people to surround themselves with—friends who would build them up and love them for who they are.

Her message stuck with me because I couldn't agree with Taylor more. When we are kids, we have complete certainty that people "grow up." We assume that as we grow physically older, others will become less hurtful and exclusive; we assume no one will be mean and everyone will act like a responsible, kind adult. Sadly, adult women still struggle with emotional wounds and low self-esteem, which leads them to hurt others. It is as if the hurt they feel spreads out to those around them.

So, as adults, how do we find safe friends who will love us just as we are? How do we walk our daughters through the pain of being left out when we are jockeying for position with mom groups that are just as exclusive? We can't encourage our kids to be inclusive and seek positive friendships if we're not modeling healthy relational patterns ourselves. We can't tell them to be themselves when we are desperately trying to impress others. We must stay true to ourselves and pursue authentic, genuine friendships, not popularity.

> We must stay true to ourselves and pursue authentic, genuine friendships, not popularity.

Elizabeth's Story

Elizabeth started coming to see me in ninth grade. She had just moved to a new school and was feeling anxious about finding a new group of friends. In middle school, Elizabeth had always been at the very top of the "status-pyramid," as my teen clients call it. Girls in her grade said she was popular because she was pretty and all of the boys had crushes on her. She also got invited to the best parties. Elizabeth didn't tell me that she was popular; rather, other clients from her school told me that they would be happy if they could only be like Elizabeth. When I would inquire why, they would say, "Because she has the best life." These clients also told me that Elizabeth lived in a beautiful house and always had the latest clothes and accessories.

Elizabeth came to me for treatment describing symptoms of anxiety. She reported feeling anxious all of the time; she only felt comfortable alone in her room. As the trust Elizabeth and I shared grew stronger, she opened up about her relationship with her mom.

Elizabeth felt enormous pressure from her mother to be popular. In second grade, her mom had told her to stop being friends with one of her closest friends because that girl wasn't in the "cool" crowd. In fourth grade, when Elizabeth was planning her birthday party, her mom pressured her to invite the girls that were "popular," even though she felt uncomfortable around them. She wanted to invite the six friends she felt closest to, but her mom reminded her that those friends were not going to get her "anywhere." Elizabeth went along with her mother's advice and invited the popular girls. After all, she didn't want to disappoint her.

Elizabeth couldn't figure out why it was so important to her mom that she be included with these girls. She didn't really feel safe with them and had other friendships that were more enjoyable. Every time she spent time with the popular girls, they talked negatively about those outside the group and put down any girl in their friend group who happened not to be there. Of course, Elizabeth assumed they talked about her when she was absent as well.

She didn't want to upset her mom, so she continued to hang out with the popular girls. Fast forward to high school, and Elizabeth was struggling to feel safe among "friends." Isn't it ironic that my other teen clients who know Elizabeth (and didn't know she was also a client) were envious, with no idea that she, too, felt insecure and less-than?

After a few sessions with Elizabeth, I asked her mom, Amy, to come in. I wanted to learn Amy's thoughts, as well as ask what she was noticing at home. Within seconds, I could sense Amy's pain and fear; I could hear her desperation. Amy was determined that

Elizabeth wouldn't feel the shame of sitting alone at lunch like she had experienced growing up.

Amy shared stories about her painful adolescence, telling of countless parties she had been excluded from and all the ways she had been teased because of her height. She vividly remembered the "friends" who deserted her when she needed them. And so, Amy put her fears on Elizabeth and completely missed how she was contributing to her daughter's anxiety.

Have you encountered these moms, the ones who desperately need their kids to fit in and engineer every aspect of their child's social life? It seems we are all little girls in grown-up bodies. We remember the pain of growing up and want to shield our girls. I get it. Who wants to watch her precious child walk through the hurt and heartache of adolescence?

The problem is, these mothers have not learned to be confident in their own skin. Perhaps in their own adolescence, they learned that being themselves was not enough. Eventually, they learned to sacrifice who they were to be someone others would include.

> We can only be free when we are willing to be ourselves.

Authenticity and Friendship

We can only be free when we are willing to be ourselves. As long as we are wearing a mask to fit in, we will feel alone—even while invited and included. People can't see us and affirm us if we give them an inauthentic façade. We will feel like we are spinning plates, trying to keep up the act, rather than settling into the comforting familiarity of being known and loved for who we really are. Popularity and acceptance built on deception is a house of cards. You can never relax. You will never reach your unique potential. So, don't buy the lie that popular is better, that popular is the way to know you are enough. Authenticity is where it's truly at.

Moms, do you expect your daughters to be popular? Is it important to you? Why? Were you popular, and it feels important that she experience the same thing? Were you unpopular, and you want to protect her from the pain of social exclusion?

At the end of the day, the quest for popularity is propelled by the fear of being alone, feeling invisible, and feeling insignificant. But can only one crowd offer us the affirmation we need? Is there only one group with the power to tell us we are worthwhile, or are there genuine friendships waiting, if we are willing to look? Can we have friends and be authentic, too?

Truth 1: There Will Always Be Cliques

Have you ever watched girl drama on a preschool playground? It is fierce. Ladies, queen bees emerge early. It's already there in preschool, for sure. I know you have seen it play out, especially if you have a daughter. You've watched as one little girl mesmerizes the others, telling them what to do, where to go, and who can play. You are left speechless as the other girls do exactly as she tells them—on cue! If only they responded that quickly to our commands! She is the boss, and they are her henchmen. We may watch with amusement or disdain, but either way, it's just the playground, right? Kids will be kids.

Now, imagine a raft in the middle of the ocean, one that fits only five people. The preschool queen bee gets to decide who will be on the raft—in her clique—and who will be pushed off to eventually drown. That scenario sounds shocking and abhorrent, right? It's no longer fun and games if the "out crowd" actually drowns! Well, social anxiety and shame can make girls feel like they can't breathe, like they won't make it out alive. Is it any wonder we compromise our authenticity to be declared "in"?

Let's consider elementary school. Who's on or off the raft is confusing. Girls wonder, *Is she my friend? Is she not my friend? We play together at recess, but she didn't invite me to her birthday party. I sit with her at lunch, but she always chooses other friends to have over to her house.* Girls this age will ignore you, even when they claim to be your friend. If they are mad at you, they won't tell you why. Often, they won't admit that they are mad but will instead say something cutting or rude and then pretend they are joking. Or, as they get older, they will say hurtful things to friends or to you via text.

You move into middle school or high school, and social media begins. Whereas before you felt confused about where you stood, now you know. You think, *I am clearly not her friend. If I was, why would she have invited these other girls to the movie (there they are, posed right in front of the movie sign) but not me?* Girls are constantly finding out about the events they were not included in via social media, and it can be confusing, humiliating, and stressful. Friends drop each other to climb higher in social status, and it is a rare blessing to find friends who are safe and reliable.

Social status is everything to those who desire the power of popularity and feel the need to play the game. Rosalind Wiseman, in *Queen Bees and Wannabees*, points out that "girls would rather put up with being treated like dirt than be alone."[15] As human beings, we pay a price to be connected, and the beehive mentality lasts into adulthood. While I wish it were true that hurtful beehive games ended in teenage years, they don't.

---

15   Rosalind Wiseman, *Queen Bees and Wannabes: Helping Your Daughter Survive Cliques, Gossip, Boys, and the New Realities of Girl World* (New York: Harmony Books, 2002).

As adults, the same dynamics show up, and we may still be jockeying for a place on the life-saving raft—one with limited seating. Without spending time in self-reflection, defining what true friendship should look like for you, you will inevitably stay locked in the popularity game. Most people aim for the "cool" raft because of our human need to connect with others, because of our natural desire to feel like we are a part of something and not alone. Some people choose it because they associate status and popularity with power. The higher your social status, the more likely you are to get included and be admired.

The raft is real. You can see it at work in neighborhoods. In workplaces. In churches. In our kids' schools, PTA/PTO events, and sports teams. Everyone is fighting for a place on the raft. You think I am kidding? Just ask someone who is not on the raft who the "cool" groups are in the neighborhood. Or who the "cool small groups" are in your church; you have no idea how many people feel excluded in a place that is supposed to feel like a safe refuge. Or ask who the "cool parents" are at your kids' school. The desperate need to get up on that raft doesn't end, my friend. The good news is, you don't have to be a part of that game. Now keep in mind, not all rafts are cliques. If you have a close group of friends that you feel known and loved by, wonderful. The question becomes, are you being yourself on the raft, or are you feeling pressure to conform to their standards and expectations? Find your people. Just make sure you get to be yourself.

Truth 2: It's Better to Be Alone Than Untrue to Yourself

Have you ever tolerated unhealthy relationships because, deep down, you'd rather be included than face being alone? Have you ever flailed and thrashed about in the water to keep your place on the "right" raft, rather than suffer being adrift for a while on your own? How much pain have you endured through the years in your quest to feel okay about who you are associated with? You may remember dumping a friend in middle or high school to reach for a "cooler group." Or you might have been the one who felt the pain of not knowing where to sit at lunch.

We all bear scars from navigating friendships and social groups. It's part of growing up and figuring out how to do life. However, continuing to let popularity and social status rule your self-worth as an adult will keep you stuck. It keeps you from living the life you are created for.

When we were growing up, we learned how to conform to keep a seat on the raft. We learned the rules, and some of us decided that playing by them was a better choice than paying attention to the way we were treated or the way we treated others. What is amazing to me is how many women stay stuck in this same mind-set past adolescence. They are willing to be treated poorly or misuse others to feel secure. But the truth is, it is a fake security. You never know how the game will go, how long you'll have a seat on the raft, or when you will get pushed off. In other words, it's not worth playing the game if it requires you to give up your authenticity to win the approval of popular others.

When we give our power to the beehive or the raft, we give control to the women who run them. We are letting their approval set the course for our behavior. We are worshiping them and their approval instead of God and his approval. We will gain the world (popularity, approval, likes, invitations), but we will lose our soul (Matt. 16:26). He created you as a unique being, not just some cog in the popularity wheel.

Ladies, we are free. We don't have to play the popularity game anymore. *You* don't have to play the game anymore. It is okay to let go of friends who aren't safe and who don't have your back. It is better to swim for a little while by yourself than to be treated poorly on the raft (or to treat someone else poorly to protect your position).

I know. You remember what it feels like to sit on the outside. You remember the pain. Growing up, we didn't have many choices. We were stuck doing life with those in our school or in our hometown. Today, we have more choices and more ways to connect than ever before. There's not one "cool" raft. In fact, we can choose to let go of the raft and channel our energy toward personal growth and unique passions. What could you accomplish if you weren't giving your power to the queen bee on the wrong raft?

> What could you accomplish if you weren't giving your power to the queen bee on the wrong raft?

Truth 3: You Can't Find the Right Friends Hanging on to the Wrong Ones

Often, we miss positive, encouraging relationships because we are trying so desperately to hang on to the wrong friends. We wonder, *What if I let go and never find other friends? What if I take this risk and find that no one else will accept me?* We are so terrified to let go that we miss all of the other wonderful connections waiting to be discovered.

But, trust me; an endless variety of rafts is available; sisterhoods of young moms, career girls, and empty nesters are out there. You will find your niche if you are willing to put popularity aside and vulnerably offer your true self.

> You will find your niche if you are willing to put popularity aside and vulnerably offer your true self.

But here is the challenge: you must let go of fake friends before you can find your people. And that takes strength and courage. You will see pictures posted of the old raft without you; you will hear how much fun they are having and how great life is. But

> You can only be free and be yourself when you have abandoned the quest for popularity.

that is when you will remember this: you can only be free and be yourself when you have abandoned the quest for popularity.

Do This Instead: Work Towards Acceptance

1. Assess Your Friendships

Ladies, we are not on *Survivor* or *Big Brother*. We do *not* have to form alliances to stay in the house or not get voted off of the island. Believe me, some people will make you feel like you need to control and manipulate and pull strings to secure social superiority. It's just not true.

Move on if your friends are sucking the life out of you. Move on if they are demeaning, insulting, or fake. Move on if they are jealous of your success or put down your accomplishments. Definitely move on if your time with them always turns to negative talk about others. If they are quick to devalue others, how can you feel safe? Women who put down other women announce, out loud, that their focus is on competition, rather than personal growth. I don't know about you, but I don't have time for competition with friends. I want to be wise with my time and use it to bear fruit, work on me, and get me closer to my best life. Therefore, I only want friends who support and celebrate each other's growth and are doing their own work, too.

2. Examine What You Want

Before you start looking for friendships that best suit you, search your soul. Figure out who you are. Think about what you want. Identify what makes you amazing. Decide what you need and what you can offer. You don't need to play the popularity game to feel whole. Endless possibilities for success and significance are available to you. Don't buy the lie that successful women have one type of look, a handful of approved interests, or a certain type of schedule and priorities. Don't sell your originality for fitting in.

3. Determine Who Your Tribe Is and Be Open

Your people are out there. True friends will love and include you. They will encourage you and empower you. True friends are excited for your wins and show up with hugs or a glass of wine for your losses. They don't need you to carry them, and they don't rely on you to solve their problems. True friends give you life and make you feel wonderful about yourself.

> True friends give you life and make you feel wonderful about yourself.

Friends, mean girls might stand out in high school, but kind women stand out for the rest of life. Surround yourself with kind women.

Reflection Questions:

1. When has the desperation to fit in led you to the wrong raft?
2. Which friendships suck the life out of you? Why haven't you set boundaries or let them go?
3. Who are three people in your life you can be yourself around? Do they know how special they are to you?

New Insight:

_____

_____

_____

_____

_____

_____

_____

_____

_____

_____

_____

Myth 12

I Should Stop When I Feel Afraid

Do one thing every day that scares you.
–Eleanor Roosevelt

What would you do if you weren't afraid? I had the privilege of hearing author Bob Goff speak on fear. "Fear is a punk," he said. And he is right. Fear is a punk. It paralyzes us and tricks us into believing lies that keep us stuck. I believe it's the enemy's most powerful weapon because it keeps us from the risks that will open up our true potential. It keeps us too anxious to share our gifts with the world. Often, we don't see fear as the true culprit, the root of our troubles; we don't realize we are letting this primal emotion stop us from living the present moment to its fullest. Our default mode is to look at the circumstances around us and blame our troubles on something or someone else. But to reach greatness, we must become aware of and then tame fear, our true enemy and the barrier to greatness.

One of our most effective tactics in fighting fear is to remember that fear is temporary. In the moment, fear feels like all there is and ever will be. We let past trauma and future worries keep us paralyzed. We roll out the welcome mat for anxiety, playing and replaying all the worst-case scenarios.

A German proverb says, "Fear makes the wolf bigger than he is." It's true; fear exaggerates reality. Is fear a punk that's been tricking and deceiving you? Have you let it run your life and control your choices? Have you believed its lies, foretelling your own doom?

In *The Body Keeps the Score*, Bessel Van der Kolk describes a study conducted by Steve Maier and Martin Seligman in 1967, which demonstrated the idea of learned helplessness by repeatedly administering electric shock to dogs locked in cages.[16] Dogs learned early on that the cages were locked and accepted their seemingly inescapable fate. However, after administering several courses of electric shock, the researchers opened the doors of the cages and then shocked the dogs again. A group of control dogs who had never been shocked before immediately ran away when the cages were opened, but the dogs who had earlier been subjected to inescapable shock made no attempt to flee, even when the door was wide open. They just lay there, as if there was no solution or escape.

The mere opportunity to escape does not make traumatized animals—or people—take the road to freedom. Like Maier and Seligman's dogs, many traumatized people simply give up. Van der Kolk writes, "Rather than risk experimenting with new options, [people] stay stuck in the fear they know."[17] Van Der Kolk also quotes his former teacher Elvin Semrad on the human response

---

16 Bessel Van der Kolk, *The Body Keeps the Score: Brain, Mind, and Body in the Healing of Trauma* (New York: Penguin, 2015).

17 Van der Kolk, 30.

to pain: "The greatest sources of our suffering are the lies we tell ourselves."[18]

Friends, that is the power of fear: it keeps us stuck and tells us we have no other options.

Kate's Story: Combating the What Ifs

Kate was a student at a local university. She came to counseling not knowing what to do with her life. She felt an enormous amount of pressure from her parents to become a doctor, but she was really interested in art history. Her parents allowed her to minor in art history, but they wanted her to choose a profession that would make her successful in their eyes. She wanted their approval, so she went along with their suggested career. She acknowledged that she would be happy being a doctor, but what terrified her is that she might study pre-med but not make it into med school.

In our first session, Kate shared that she was an extreme perfectionist. She recalled her years in elementary school as stressful because she never wanted to fail. She told the story of coming in second in the school spelling bee. Even though she was in third grade, going up against a fifth grader, she still blamed herself for not winning. It didn't help that her parents told her she should have practiced more.

She loved to dance and chose to pursue ballet at an early age. She later wondered about trying a different style of dance, but she was afraid to look foolish by becoming a novice in another style. Besides, her parents thought classical ballet was the only dance worth her time. Kate also considered running for a leadership role in school as she loved organizing events. But, she worried about losing, unsure if she could handle the disappointment.

---

18   Van der Kolk, 26-27.

While a straight-A student in high school, Kate struggled with anxiety. She had an overwhelming fear of failure, even though all evidence pointed to her aptitude and abilities. When it came time to apply to college, she could have received a scholarship and been accepted to a number of different collegiate institutions, but she only applied to one—the safe choice. As you can imagine, she was concerned about what would happen if she wasn't accepted.

Kate definitely had a case of the "what-ifs." In fact, it sounded to me like much of her life had been controlled by the fear of what might go wrong, prove disappointing, or feel uncomfortable. She wondered, *What if I choose the wrong university? What if I choose the wrong major? What if I choose the wrong roommate? What if I join a sorority and hate it? What if I don't join a sorority and regret it?*

Kate's life was completely run by fear. Instead of focusing on ways to soar, she fixated on not failing. To explore the anxiety, Kate and I created a list with two columns. We titled the left side "What If" and the other side "Then." You can do this at home with a few of your most overwhelming fears, by the "If/Then Chart" I've provided in the appendix. On the left side, we listed the struggles that led her to counseling. On the right side, we finished the thought and considered the possible outcomes:

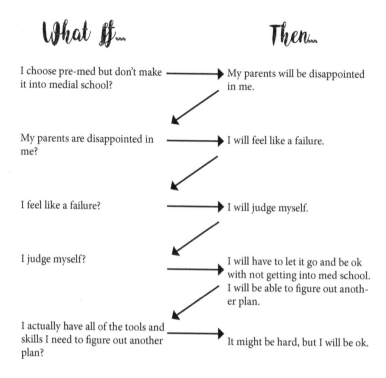

An If/Then Chart helps us spot and question irrational thoughts. Too often, we catastrophize the what-if and make it a bigger deal than it deserves to be. When we examine the "then" that follows, we often realize we can handle it. This chart can also be useful in considering what things might look like six months after the fear comes true as you envision how you might resourcefully handle the fallout of the event you fear most. You could also list the pros and cons of holding on to the what-if, comparing its perceived protective factors against the actual cost of letting fear hold you back.

Once Kate walked through the exercise, she realized she had the tools and skills to face the outcome and control what happened next. She was able to believe she could devise another plan if she didn't make it into med school. While it wouldn't be what she wanted, she would be okay. She realized one bad outcome wouldn't wreck her life. Over time, she may even come to believe that undesired events and outcomes can actually prepare her for the future and grow her into all she is meant to be.

Truth 1: Most of What We Fear Is a Fantasy

Our primal brain was designed to look for fear and scan for threats in the environment. Some call it our reptilian brain because we have this area of our brain (our brain stem) in common with some of the most basic creatures on earth. However, God also gave humans a very advanced prefrontal cortex. This brain region can make rational decisions and see both the good and bad in any circumstance. What would happen if you stopped living from your reptilian brain, scanning for danger and being stuck in reactive mode? What could you accomplish if you stopped analyzing what could go wrong and instead focused on what could go right? Engage the part of your brain that is able to see gradients of hope and probability. Yes, bad things happen, but so do good things, and often events turn out better than you could have imagined. So, focus on the positive and give your very best to the process.

We get more of what we focus on, so focus on the possibilities. Please, I beg you. Stop letting your what-ifs get in the way of walking toward your dreams. Stop giving your power away to unlikely possibilities and focus on the beauty that could come from stepping out in faith.

Truth 2: Only You Can Push You Past Your Fear

As adults, we don't have parents, friends, teachers, or coaches forcing us to step out and push for our dreams. It is up to us to push past fear and pursue possibility. We must find inner motivation to leave the comfort of certainty for the risk of the unknown. True, life offers no guarantees, and we can't predict success or failure. But, remember, it is okay to fail. Failure is actually a good thing as it allows us to get up, learn from our mistakes, and ultimately fly higher than we ever imagined.

The hardest part of pursuing your dream is summoning the courage to quell the fear, step out, and try. That first step requires bravery and pluck and can only happen once we've become sick and tired of being stuck. Moving

> Moving forward requires us to see fear for what it is: an obstacle to our greatness.

forward requires us to see fear for what it is: an obstacle to our greatness. We can only be courageous if we look fear in the eye and accept that even though failure is a possible outcome, we will survive and live to try again.

Do This Instead: Work Towards Courage

1. Face the Fear

Risk. Step out. Show up. Be vulnerable. We are powerful not because we don't have fear but because we push through the fear and go on in spite of it. Exciting new research is proving that phobias and even some forms of trauma respond well to gradated exposure therapy. In a controlled environment, one can experience elements of the feared situation or object. In many cases, exposure therapy works better and faster than talk therapy alone. So, what's our real-life takeaway? Just thinking about your fear or even talking through it may never bring about the degree of change you need. You may have to face fear head-on.

As you prepare to step into uncomfortable places, reframe fear as excitement and anticipation. Be mindful of your increased adrenaline and energy and channel it into your mission. Know that it will get easier the more you bring fear out into the light and expose it as a punk and a liar.

Your growth and success are 100 percent up to you. No one else can do it for you, and no one else is to blame if you hang back and stay stuck. Acting is the only thing that will move you forward. Take a look at your past choices and dominate life patterns and reflect on ways that fear has kept you small. Then, do the thing you fear. Greatness is waiting.

(Note: If you are a victim of trauma, please seek professional help to determine the best way to explore past pain and present fears in a stable, grounded environment. Do not attempt exposure therapy alone if your fears are the result of abuse or tragedy.)

2. Act As If You're Confident

No. I am not saying be fake. If you believe you are worthy and have something to offer, then you are not disingenuous in portraying confidence. You may begin with acting "as if" you are confident, even if you are not completely there yet. It's okay to pretend or act at first because confidence is a skill—and you can sharpen that skill. When you act as if you are confident, people respond to you as a confident person, which, in turn, makes you more confident. If you act bravely, you will feel brave. Try it. You will be amazed!

When you enter a new or uncomfortable situation, ask yourself how you might act differently if you were the most confident person in the room. Then do that. Don't waste time and energy wondering if you are good enough. You are good enough. You are enough. Now, behave like it!

3. Embrace Fear

Talk about fear. Bring it out of the shadows and take away its power. Have the courage to share your imperfect, broken story of what fear looks like for you and how you are battling your way through it. Be real with others and talk about how it feels to live with the tension fear creates for you. Model what it looks like to stop fearing failure. Demonstrate messy and imperfect progress. Over time, fear will lose its power to limit you or slow you down. And, you'll win the respect of those around you as you give voice to a common emotion that is all too often suffered in silence.

Reflection Questions:

1. How does fear show up in the story of your life?
2. What might you try if you could push past your fear?
3. If you saw yourself as powerful and capable, how would your thoughts change? Which thoughts would you eliminate?

New Insight:

_____

_____

_____

_____

_____

_____

_____

_____

_____

_____

_____

_____

I Am the Only One Who Feels So Alone

Loneliness and the feeling of being unwanted
is the most terrible poverty.

–MOTHER TERESA

Strong relationships are a crucial component in a full and meaningful life. Without human connection, we feel empty, sad, and depleted. Knowing we have someone in our corner soothes our primal need to belong and feel protected.

Technology has produced more opportunities for social connection than we ever dreamed possible. Ironically, loneliness rates are at an all-time high. Reports state that loneliness is a new epidemic.[19] We see images of people and their comments online all day, every day, but that kind of contact doesn't connect us. We send dozens of texts but never hear our friend's voice. We watch sermons online and get lazy about coming together as a church body.

---

19   Fiza Pirani, "Why Are Americans So Lonely? Massive Study Finds Nearly Half of US Feels Alone, Young Adults Most of All," *The Atlanta Journal-Constitution*, May 1, 2018.

But being lonely doesn't necessarily mean being alone. Have you ever felt lonely at a concert or sporting event? You were surrounded by people who obviously shared a common interest, yet you felt disconnected. We can actually feel the loneliest when we are amongst a crowd if we sense a disconnect between the mood of the crowd and our feelings inside. We may think, *I am the only one who feels sad right now. I am the only one who came here tonight with problems.*

Loneliness can actually be a very helpful feeling if we understand it as a sign. Loneliness signals that we need relationship.[20] It's a reminder that we need others to walk through life with. Our sense of wellness depends on knowing we matter, feeling we are seen, and trusting we belong. When we feel a headache coming on, we reach for Tylenol. When we feel loneliness, we must reach for connection. It's the cure for what ails us.

Unfortunately, we live in a world of digital media that offers counterfeit connection. It seems safer to tweet or post; we are saved the hassle and vulnerability of showing up in person. At home, you can take twenty shots before you capture your best look to post. You can revise and reword your update until it is flawless. There's less room for error in your carefully edited virtual world. And, there's a shot of dopamine when the likes start rolling in, giving you a false sense of community and acceptance.

For all the connection it promises, social media can definitely exacerbate feelings of loneliness, anxiety, and depression.

Alas, the feeling of acceptance can be fleeting as social media sometimes reminds us that we don't

---

20   Chip Dodd, *The Voice of the Heart: A Call to Full Living* (Los Olivos, CA: Sage Hill, 2001), 53.

belong. We see events we missed and friends who seem to be having more fun. We witness the benchmarks others are reaching and feel ashamed we haven't achieved that same level of success. It's hard to look at pictures of your neighbor's Caribbean vacation when you just got an overdraft notice from the bank. For all the connection it promises, social media can definitely exacerbate feelings of loneliness, anxiety, and depression.

No wonder we feel so alone and messed up.

Kara's Story: Reconnecting After Loss

Kara was a single mom of two young girls, ages seven and five. She lost her husband to cancer a year before coming to counseling. His diagnosis came a year after they moved away from family in Chicago for his new job in the health care industry in Nashville. They spent three years going from doctor appointments to chemo and radiation treatments before he finally lost the fight.

After her husband passed, Kara worked from home as an account executive for an online insurance company and spent most of her days dealing with angry customers while her children were at school or day care. She spent her evenings trying to keep her children happy and fed.

Kara's parents wanted her to move back to Chicago, now that she was raising the girls alone, but she worried about moving them again after all of the change they had experienced in losing their dad. Her sister, brother, and their families were in Chicago as well, making it tempting to move back home. Even though proximity to family sounded comforting, Kara also shared that she and her sister struggled relationally; being near her might not be so helpful. She felt like her sister had always relied heavily on her, but she just didn't have much to give after her loss.

Kara was living in a large neighborhood full of young families. She walked her girls to school in the morning and saw other families but didn't know how to connect. Her girls were shy and never ran up to the other kids or created opportunities for conversation. She would've liked to have other kids over to play more often, but as a working single mom, she just couldn't find the time.

When she walked into the neighborhood pool, she immediately felt insecure. She didn't know where to sit as she noticed "closed" friend groups of women everywhere she looked. No one ever invited her to sit with them, even though they would smile and say a polite hello.

She tried to connect with women she had met in the neighborhood but couldn't seem to get past surface conversation. She invited some of the women over for dinner, but they never reciprocated. Kara said she had one friend she met after moving to Tennessee, but the friend stopped engaging with her. She self-reflected to examine if she had done something wrong, but she just couldn't make sense of it.

Kara was active in her church when her husband was alive, but after his passing, she felt she didn't have a place. The singles group seemed like a dating pool, something that she was not ready for, but those in couples groups acted awkward around her.

Kara came in feeling depressed, anxious, and worried about the future. Underneath those understandable feelings was a great deal of loneliness. She didn't know who was in her corner. She didn't know who had her back or who she could rely on. She longed to have friends who were safe, reliable, and authentic. She just didn't know where or how to find them.

Truth 1: There Are Billions of People Here with You

If I hear one theme over and over in my office, it is that of loneliness, exclusion, and rejection. These forces burn deep into our soul, making us certain we are insignificant and small. The truth is, loneliness is just a feeling; it is not a fact. It is an emotion, and it will pass.

When you feel loneliness creeping in, take a deep breath and remember the people God has placed in your life. You are not alone. Who can you call? Who can you ask to lunch? Who can remind you that you are seen and known? You may be surprised to find that those you reach out to were in need of companionship as well. How often do we all suffer in silence instead of reaching out and giving the gift of friendship to others who need it, too?

Often, loneliness is a result of busyness and skewed priorities. Have you pushed social connection to the side in the name of productivity? You can likely get back into fulfilling relationships with just a little effort. Learn to balance your to-do list with downtime that fosters relationship. You must create margin if you expect to fellowship with others. Loneliness can simply mean you haven't taken the time or the risk to meet new people in a while.

> At our deepest core, we need a sense of significance and acceptance—fostered by our relationship with God and others.

Truth 2: We All Need to Be Seen, Heard, and Loved

While we may neglect our social side for a season, we can't keep up that pattern for long. We need people. We need face-to-face contact. At our deepest core, we need a sense of significance and acceptance—fostered by our relationship with God and others. Feeling down and depressed when you are lonely isn't crazy. It's quite natural. You were made to be seen, heard, and loved. It is not selfish to want time with others. It is crucial for your well-being.

As author Chip Dodd says, "Loneliness renders us vulnerable to our hunger for emotional and spiritual fulfillment, thus exposing us to all relationship needs. But in a world that screams negativity about dependency and glorifies self-sufficiency, loneliness is the feeling that we work hardest to avoid. The irony is that the more we work to avoid it, the more it occurs. And the more we work to hide it, the more we miss out on life."[21] Honor the loneliness you feel. Admit your need for others. Embrace the part of you that wants to connect, contribute, and commit to relationship. You are not alone in feeling lonely sometimes!

> You were made to be seen, heard, and loved.

Do This Instead: Work Towards Connection

1. Embrace Learning Something New

One of the best ways to feel connected is to join a group or a class. Joining a class allows you to meet people in a comfortable, relaxed way. None of us want to walk up to someone out of the blue in a random place and ask if she would like to be our friend. Nor do we want anyone to try that with us!

Friendships begin organically in common space: work, gyms, kid events, hobby activities, churches, and other shared interests. If you love photography and take a class, you will likely connect with the other enthusiasts. If you join a fitness class, it will eventually seem natural to suggest grabbing coffee afterwards. If you live in a neighborhood, options could include playdates at

---

21   Chip Dodd, *The Voice of the Heart: A Call to Full Living* (Los Olivos, CA: Sage Hill, 2001).

the park, jogging groups, wine tasting clubs, dog walking groups, cooking clubs, book clubs, Bible studies, etc. You might also explore opportunities to connect with others while volunteering and serving your community. The possibilities are endless. Show up. Be seen. And be known.

2. Embrace a New Chapter

Seasons come and go in life, and sometimes feeling lonely is exactly what we need to be prepared for the next chapter. Think about the caterpillar. He lives a life of community with his fuzzy friends until one day he finds himself cocooning. He goes inward and focuses on who he needs to be. It is lonely in that cocoon, but if he doesn't go through the process of drawing inward, he can't turn into who he is created to be: a beautiful butterfly. Without that time alone, the world would miss out on the full expression of his beauty.

Could you use your loneliness as a way to discover and examine who you are becoming as you head into your next chapter? Could you focus on future dreams and goals instead of what feels uncomfortable right now? Could you go back to school and take those courses you've always thought about? Could you get a part-time job that would align with your interests or passions? Could you create a blog that might speak to others walking through a similar experience? Could you examine what gives you energy and where your passions lie?

Use the space loneliness allows to recalibrate and move with intention and purpose toward the life you desire.

3. Address Your Negative Self-Talk

As I mentioned in our discussion of myth 4, "If I Feel That Way, It Must Be True," it's important to ask, "What is the story I am telling myself? When does it show up and how does it serve me?"

Ladies, are you lonely because you are truly alone or because you are holding back from relationship, telling yourself you are unworthy and unlovable? If you've just moved to a new town or suddenly have more free time to cultivate friendships, then, yes, let's devise a plan to move toward connection. But what if you are alone because you've let insecurity control your calendar? What if negative self-talk has convinced you that you have nothing to offer and every perceived slight is intentional and deserved?

It may take time and require effort, but you must learn to love yourself before you can expect others to love you and connect with you. Remember, you are Abba's child (Rom. 8:15) and have a unique contribution to offer. Don't buy the lie that you are lonely because you deserve to be or because you are uninteresting or lack value. The negative self-talk must go if you want to build authentic friendships.

> It may take time and require effort, but you must learn to love yourself before you can expect others to love you and connect with you.

4. Break Down the Walls

Or perhaps you are alone because your walls are up and you aren't receptive to the connection easily available to you. Now, I am not insinuating that you are making up the feeling of loneliness you struggle with. However, it's worth asking: are others reaching out to you yet coming up against a wall? The wall may have been crucial for keeping you safe at another stage in your life, when unsafe people hurt you. The wall protected you from additional pain. People don't build walls unless they have to. I get it. But sometimes the need for the extra protection passes, yet we keep our defenses up. Thus, these walls keep us from experiencing true connection with others. What was once a means of protection could now be a limitation.

It might be painful to read that *you* could be part of the reason that you are lonely. We are all prone to getting in our own way. Well, maybe you don't, but I sure do! When I am in my own way, it is usually because I am telling myself a story that isn't true.

Being open and vulnerable is risky. I understand that hiding behind the wall feels safer, but I encourage you to examine the long-term cost of hiding versus the benefit of opening up and reaching out to form new relationships.

Listen, I'm not asking you to pole vault over the wall and jump right into a crowd of strangers. I am asking you to take a step around the wall and explore different opportunities. You never know who you will meet when you are vulnerable and show up.

Reflection Questions:

1. In which areas of life do you feel least connected to others? Why might that be so?
2. What's one step you can take to move toward community?
3. Is your loneliness a result of circumstances (a recent move or a job change) or walls you've constructed out of shame, fear, or anger? If you've built walls, how can you work through your defenses and start letting safe others in?

New Insight:

_____

_____

_____

_____

_____

_____

_____

_____

_____

_____

_____

_____

Holding a Grudge Protects Me

If we really want to love, we must first learn how to forgive.
–Mother Teresa

get it. You want them to know how badly they hurt you. I would, too.

You want them to know that the damage is severe. Absolutely. It is so severe.

You want them to hurt as badly as you do. But, they won't. That is just the way it is. Hurt people, hurt people. And the cycle continues.

When I speak to a room about the topic of forgiveness, I immediately notice body language; people tense up and their countenance changes. Their open and interested faces shift to closed and guarded. It is almost as if you can see the pain from their hurt, betrayal, abuse, fear, abandonment, or loss oozing out of their wounds while the armor they use to protect their wounds comes out in full force.

The message is clear: "Not me. I won't open myself up again to that hurt. I won't be vulnerable like that ever again."

Amy's Story: Resolving the Resentment

Amy came into my office trying to figure out how to deal with her parents. As a new mom, she was trying to figure out appropriate boundaries for her new family regarding her family of origin. She wanted her daughter to have a relationship with her parents, but when reflecting on the hurt they had caused her for years, she wasn't sure how to move forward. She wondered if she was being selfish in protecting her daughter from the same type of behavior that she endured growing up.

As we explored Amy's pain, it was clear that she grew up in a difficult family system. An only child, Amy had vivid memories of manipulation, shame, and verbal abuse from her father. She remembered him screaming at her, telling her she would never become anything important and expecting her to support his alcohol and gambling addiction by driving him to bars and casinos. When we were able to do some work surrounding her pain, she recalled excruciating memories surrounding her dad, including a time when he sold a car she had saved to buy so that he could use the money for gambling. When she reacted in anguish, he told her that she shouldn't have gotten so attached to it because things come and go in life.

Amy also remembers countless times where he would say he was going to be at her sports games, yet he left her down because he was at the bar or casino instead. There were times she thought his absence was better, even though it hurt. When he did show up at her games, he would show up drunk. He would yell at the coaches and the referees for not putting his daughter in the game.

Amy doesn't just hold anger toward her father; she holds resentment toward her mother as well. "I just can't help but wonder what life would have been like if my mom had protected me," Amy said. Her mother enabled her dad's behavior and never stood up for her. Her mom confided in Amy that she wished it would be different but shrugged it off as "just how your dad is."

After Amy moved out of the house and went to college on an academic scholarship, things changed at home. Her dad hit rock bottom when he had to file for bankruptcy due to his gambling, and her mom finally got up the courage to move out until he got himself sober. Luckily, he did.

Amy was grateful that her parents began the healing process. As part of his treatment program, her dad acknowledged his wrongdoing and asked her for her forgiveness, something she had not been able to do. Forgiveness seemed difficult because this man had caused her so much pain.

The problem was, Amy was the one holding on to the pain and negative energy. In not forgiving her dad, she kept space open for pain and hurt, expending her energy on resentment. Her inability to forgive him was like an anchor on her heart. She wanted so badly to open herself up to him. She wanted to feel his love and protection, which she longed for as a child, but she just couldn't open her heart. The cost of being vulnerable was too much of a risk.

You can probably relate to Amy's story. Can you think of a time the wound was too deep to want to forgive? Many times, the grudge seems justified. We fear letting the offender "off the hook" by forgiving. Sadly, holding the grudge causes more pain for us than for the one who's wronged us. Let's consider what's really true about grudges, forgiveness, and freedom.

Truth 1: Forgiveness Is For You

When we hold on to a grudge, or refuse to forgive someone, *we* are the one in bondage. We are the one losing energy or sleep over it, and it keeps us stuck. The other person is going on with her life, yet we are suspended in time.

Think about the amount of energy it takes to hold on to a grudge. It impacts us physically as we feel it in our bodies or our immune system. It impacts us emotionally as we replay the offense over and over and feel sad, depressed, or anxious. It impacts us relationally as we are reluctant to trust others who might also hurt

> When we hold on to a grudge, or refuse to forgive someone, *we* are the one in bondage.

us. Not forgiving someone costs us *our* freedom.

Friends, here's the truth. Forgiving someone doesn't erase the offense. It just lets you be free from the rumination and anger. It doesn't condone the behavior or say her actions were okay (they were not). It just takes the burden off our shoulders and gives it to God to take care of. Don't we all want that kind of freedom?

None of us can totally forget trauma or make life like it didn't happen. None of us can erase loss, hurt, betrayal, or abuse. Nor should we. We want to honor the feelings that came out of our past and heal from them, not continue to let them rob us of joy. When we lean in, acknowledge, find meaning in, and forgive, we are stronger.

Truth 2: Forgiveness Requires Boundaries

Forgiveness does not green-light harmful behavior or give individuals permission to continue on with reckless or inconsiderate behavior. If someone wrongs us or acts disrespectfully, we can forgive *and* establish boundaries for future interactions. Forgiveness does not mean resuming your previous unhealthy relationship.

When we forgive, we get to decide how that person shows up in our life going forward. If the offense was hurtful, but relatively minor, the relationship may be able to resume under healthier boundaries. But if the offense was catastrophic, under no circumstance should the offender be allowed in your life. You can say, no more. Remember, boundaries tell others what is okay and not okay for us in relationship. Forgiveness should never put us back into a dangerous circumstance.

Do This Instead: Work Towards Freedom

1. Ask, "What Do I Need to Let Go?"

What are you holding on to that is not serving you well? Resentment? Anger? Frustration? Are you stuck in the past, replaying the hurt, or wishing for what could have been? As long as you are withholding forgiveness, you are letting someone else occupy free space in your brain.

How are these heavy feelings showing up in your life? Do you experience emotional anguish each day? Do you have physical sensations linked to these memories? Our brains and bodies are intricately connected. Holding on to pain and choosing not to forgive can eventually make you physically ill. Autoimmune diseases and gut-related issues are two medical issues linked to stress.

Whatever you find the hardest to let go of is probably the thing you need to let go of the most. What has you under its control? More pain and more bondage is all resentment can offer. How would it feel to release that wrongdoer and surrender the grudge?

> Holding on to pain and choosing not to forgive can eventually make you physically ill. Autoimmune diseases and gut-related issues are two medical issues linked to stress.

A licensed therapist can help you process traumatic memories so that you can move forward and let go. Don't hesitate to ask for professional help. Forgiveness isn't forgetting, and it is important to have closure with the events that have troubled you. Take the time and energy needed to forgive and let go from a place of health and healing.

2. Ask, "What's the Benefit of Holding On?"

Consider this well-told story. Two Buddhist monks return to their monastery after the rains. They reach a flooded river, beside which is a beautiful woman in a delicate silk kimono, distressed because she is unable to cross the river by herself. The older monk scoops her up and carries her safely to the other side. Then the two monks continue on their way in silence.

Later, as the monks reach their destination, the younger monk—having fumed for the last five hours—finally bursts out, "How could you do it? We are not allowed to touch a woman!" The older monk, surprised, replies, "I put her down five hours ago, but you are still carrying her with you."

The things we hold on to cloud our mind and take us from the present moment. They keep us stuck. The older monk was not carrying the burden. The younger monk was, yet the older monk's action wasn't even his problem. The younger monk allowed the elder's actions to control his mood and derail his day. You will find no peace while fuming over what another has already done.

When we choose to forgive someone who has wronged us, we take away his power. We are saying, "I cannot erase the past, but I can keep you from controlling my present and my future." Remember, forgiveness doesn't mean we are condoning

> Forgiveness opens doors to new possibilities–which will be missed or passed up if we are busy looking backward.

the injustice. It does mean we will no longer be the victim. Our lives are no longer controlled by the offense, and we are free to go forward in strength and courage to be the person we are meant to be. Forgiveness opens doors to new possibilities—which will be missed or passed up if we are busy looking backward. Mahatma Gandhi is quoted as saying, "The weak can never forgive. Forgiveness is the attribute of the strong."

And, in reality, we are called to forgive. Why? Because Christ was the ultimate forgiver. He *is* forgiveness. How can we hold grudges when he doesn't hold them against us? We are called to follow his example as we live in relationship with others: "Be kind to one another, tenderhearted, forgiving one another, as God in Christ forgave you" (Eph. 4:32).

3. Apologize

Come on, ladies. We can all think of someone we have hurt, knowingly or unknowingly: a family member, a coworker, or (cringe) a friend in junior high school. You will feel free when you ask for forgiveness. It's such an essential step that Alcoholics Anonymous (AA) teaches that no one can move forward with sobriety until he has asked others to forgive his past mistakes. AA realizes the power of a clean slate, of taking responsibility for the times we have caused others pain. But, here's the thing—this step isn't only for addicts. Each of us can experience the joy of owning and confessing our wrongs.

Now, the other may not be ready to step into forgiveness, but at least you have done everything in your power to reconcile. It takes strength to say you're sorry, but it will free up energy previously apportioned to shame and regret and give you a new outlook. We can't love others well if we can't show humility and ask for forgiveness ourselves.

4. Accept That You Won't Always Receive an Apology

While you might embrace the healing and growth that comes with forgiveness, the truth is, not everyone will feel the same way. Whether it be upbringing, temperament, or current life circumstance, some are just not in a position to forgive—or apologize. Everything becomes so much easier when you accept that not everyone can give those gifts. Not everyone is doing the work you've committed to. Some haven't realized how resentment or shame is keeping them stuck.

You will have countless overdue apologies in your life, and if you hang out in negative energy space, waiting for someone to say sorry, you will be disappointed. And, you will eventually find your way back to resentment and anger. Do your part to make things right, but don't get wrapped up in the apologies you deserve. You get to do the work. You get to know the freedom that comes from forgiveness and apologizing. You are no longer in bondage, and you are no longer stuck. Rejoice.

Reflection Questions:

1. How do you approach the topic of forgiveness? Do you have positive feelings about this practice, or do you see it as unreasonable or impossible?

2. In what circumstance do you need to consider forgiving someone, even if you don't really feel like it? Do you withhold forgiveness, even while believing God has forgiven you?

3. Do you need to approach a friend, coworker, or family member and apologize for something big—or even something small—to get that relationship back on track?

New Insight:

_____

_____

_____

_____

_____

_____

_____

_____

_____

_____

Myth 15

It Is Someone Else's Job to Make Me Happy

Folks are usually about as happy as they make their minds up to be.
–Abraham Lincoln

Do you remember playing games with your girlfriends at recess in elementary school? I remember playing games like M.A.S.H., a game designed to predict who you would marry, how many kids you would have, what type of car you would drive, and if you would live in a Mansion, Apartment, Shack, or House. I never focused on the details of these predictions, but I did know that I wanted to be "happy."

Ah, happiness. It's something we all long for, yet it seems so difficult to find. We search for it in food, relationships, retail stores, restaurants, wine bottles, and social media posts. And these things outlets often offer a temporary reprieve from pain. But long term, we come up empty. The hollow part we tried to fill with "happy" still remains.

With more resources than ever, why are so many struggling to find authentic happiness? (Note: In this chapter I am not referring to individuals who struggle with clinical depression or other mental illness).

Andrea's Story: A Happiness Project

Andrea began working with me because she wanted to be "happy." She shared that she hadn't felt happy in years and couldn't understand why. Her marriage of fifteen years was "okay" but lacked real passion or intimacy. She complained that her husband worked long hours as a police officer, and she wished he was home more. She also mentioned that she wished they had more income so she could buy material items her friends had; she felt a pressing need to keep up with her friends. Ultimately, Andrea feared losing relationships if she couldn't spend money the way her friends could.

Her three children were healthy and developmentally on track, but she was upset that they weren't straight-A students. Being a teacher herself, she feared other people would think less of her if her kids weren't on the honor roll.

She was a second-grade teacher, and while she loved her students, she stated that, in reality, she regretted going directly from college into the classroom as she wonders if she might've been better suited for a different profession. She doesn't want to change jobs now because she is happy to have her summers off, but she complained of the challenges she deals with at school, like test-performance pressure in her district and demanding parents.

Andrea felt frustrated because she wanted to lose weight and felt like she had very little time to devote to exercise between her various roles as mom, wife, and teacher. She gained thirty pounds when her youngest child was born and hadn't found a way to get it off. She had tried fad diets, but nothing worked. She joined the gym but never found time to go.

Andrea felt stuck in loneliness and desperately wanted to feel connected with other women. However, after experiencing many hurtful relationships, she found it difficult to trust people. As a result, her relationships were mostly surface level. Believing she had to meet certain standards to be worthy of friendship, she kept everyone at a distance to avoid getting hurt.

No wonder Andrea was unhappy! She was expecting other people and her circumstances to make her happy. Her husband needed to make more money. She needed status and possessions to feel secure in her friendships. Her children needed to make better grades. Her job needed to feel less demanding. She needed more free time to exercise. She believed she was stuck until these external factors changed, dismissing the internal work that needed to be done. She didn't recognize her own role in the process of getting unstuck and becoming happier.

I was honored to help Andrea evaluate what was true about happiness and what was not. After some reflection, she learned to take responsibility for her own happiness and to stop waiting for others to create it. Andrea realized that she was stuck as long as she was looking to others to create her happiness.

Truth 1: Happiness Is a Choice

Friends, we all wake up every day and have a choice. You must decide: will I be happy, or will I focus on what is flawed? I know that sounds harsh, but it is true. Happiness begins and ends in your mind. If you tell yourself you are having a bad day, then you are having a bad day. If you tell yourself no one likes you, then others' words and actions will be filtered through that belief. If you tell yourself you are unattractive, then, yep, you'll feel unlovable.

> Happiness begins and ends in your mind.

We can choose to be happy, regardless of our circumstances, or we can choose to feel sad, even in an ideal situation. The day turns on this decision.

You deserve to be happy. You deserve to feel joy. Don't let others get you off track and certainly don't allow your own thoughts to sabotage your day. People who claim happiness don't have perfect lives; they just focus on the beautiful parts. Happiness isn't external; it is internal, formed by where you choose to turn your inner gaze and by the inner dialogue you decide to indulge.

Truth 2: Happiness Is Your Responsibility

Guess what? *You* are responsible for your own happiness. Not your circumstances. Not your bank account. Not your family. Not your friends. Not your spouse and, certainly, not your kids. Imagine the power you are giving away when you expect someone else to manage your emotions. You are powerless when you allow your mood to be set by circumstance.

Happiness is being filled with joy, regardless of circumstances. We cannot control what comes at us in life, but we can control how we respond and the way we let it impact us. When we are filled up with the Spirit and embrace God's love and joy, we don't have to look to loved ones or favorable (but transient) events to provide our happiness. We have a rock-solid source of support, rather than a life built on shifting sand (Matt. 7:24-27).

> Happiness is being filled with joy, regardless of circumstances.

Truth 3: Happiness Comes with Letting Go

Much of life's stress is generated by unmet expectations. When relationships or circumstances fall short of our (often unrealistic and unexpressed) desires, we are disappointed and become resentful. Disappointment equals our expectations divided by reality.

$$Disappointment = \frac{Expectation}{Reality}$$

We must use wisdom to clarify what is realistic to expect and what cravings will only bring us grief. This is true for what we expect of ourselves and what we want from others. Once we identify the unrealistic expectations and unjust demands, the next step is to let it go. Just release yourself, others, and your environment from always living up to your high standards. Where is there resentment in your life? With whom are you angry for not meeting your unspoken requests? What do you need to let go of today?

Once you adjust your expectations, I recommend creating a separate gratefulness journal to write down all you already have to be grateful for. Giving thanks for what you have is a positive step toward letting go of what is out of your control. Learn to be mindful in the moment. Breathe deeply and be thankful for what is. Surrender perfectionistic standards and irrational demands.

Do This Instead: Work Towards Joy

1. Examine Your Expectations

Disappointment = expectations/reality. Expectations are powerful, and unmet expectations will get us every time. We usually don't even realize we have expectations until we are angry they weren't fulfilled. Our assumptions can be subtle and covert, slipping into our mind as we indulge in the fantasy of what things will be like "when." And then BAM. Disappointment rocks us when reality is less than the best-case scenario. When things don't often turn out exactly how we hoped they'd be, disappointment can gain a foothold.

A common area of disappointed is when we expect other people to behave as we would or as we think they should. Have you ever constructed a dream storyline only to be blindsided by reality? Here are a few examples:

- "I am going to love our new neighbors." And then you don't.
- "My husband will always be there for me." And then he's not.
- "My kids will be straight-A students." And then they struggle.
- "She's going to be my best friend." And then she's not.

What if we reworked these with a splash of grat-real-ity (a mix of graitutde and reality):

- "I might like the new neighbors, but it is okay if we don't connect." And it is okay.
- "My husband loves me, but he is an imperfect human, as we all are, and is doing the best he can." And it is okay.
- "My kids are valuable and wonderful, regardless of their capability in school. I just hope they give their best, and everything else will fall into place." And it does.
- "I really enjoy spending time with her and am thankful we can have a friendship." And it works.

If you are unhappy with the way things are in your life, change them or change your focus. Of course, some things in life are unchangeable. I can't make myself taller. But I can refuse to focus on something I can't change. I can choose to accept that I am always going to be 5' 3" and then focus on personal variables I have more control over, like cultivating patience or getting more sleep. As former author and speaker Jim Rohn has been quoted to say, "If you don't like how things are, change it!"

2. Serve or Volunteer

When we are serving others, we can't help but feel better ourselves. Service brings out happiness and creates connections and community. We enjoy an increased sense of belonging when working toward a common goal, which increases our positive feelings. Those who volunteer their time receive a boost in self-esteem, knowing that they are contributing to the well-being of others.

According to a 2013 survey by the United Health Group, 96 percent of people who volunteered over the last twelve months said that volunteering increased their sense of purpose; 94 percent of the respondents in the same study said that volunteering improved their mood.[22] Purposeful people are happy people. The more you focus on helping others in need, the less time you have to fret over what is not ideal in your own life. And, volunteering with disadvantaged populations might give you a reality check; you may realize you already have more than enough to rejoice and be glad.

3. Stop Comparing

While comparing our life to the less fortunate, we are reminded of all we have. However, as I mentioned in myth 2, "Other People's Lives Are So Much Better," comparing ourselves to neighbors or those in our social circles will most likely drain us of our joy. It is

---

22   https://www.unitedhealthgroup.com/content/dam/UHG/PDF/2013/UNH-Health-Volunteering-Study.pdf.

really difficult to feel happy when focusing on what we don't have and how things should have gone. When we compare life as it is to life as we hoped it would be, nothing is ever enough. We are never enough. We focus on lack instead of abundance. Ladies, we all have the power to shift our focus. And focusing on disappointment and comparison will never make us happy.

A recent tweet from Bob Goff reads, "We won't be distracted with comparison if we are captivated with purpose." Do you know why horses wear blinders over their eyes when they are racing? It is so they don't look over at the horse in the next lane to see who is winning. If a horse looks to the right, he will stumble and fall. It is essential that he keep looking ahead. It is essential that we keep looking ahead, too. Not to the right, not to the left. Not at our friend's new car. Not at her beautiful house. Not at the perfect marriage. Look ahead. Look up at God. Jesus is the only person we should be comparing ourselves to.

Gratitude is a powerful discipline. It calms our nervous system and creates peace in our hearts. It creates open space for us to step into possibility and embrace new things. Disappointment is just disappointment. It is okay to be disappointed. Hope, but don't expect. Holding loosely to expectations will keep us from spiraling into sadness when a situation doesn't work out the way we think it should. Instead, be in the moment. Live in today. Be happy and grateful for your blessings. Serve those in need. Love God and love others.

Reflection Questions:

1. How do you define *happiness*? Are your expectations realistic?
2. What would happiness look like if you could accept things you can't control?
3. In what areas can you eliminate distractions that keep you from living on purpose?

New Insight:

_____

_____

_____

_____

_____

_____

_____

_____

_____

_____

_____

_____

Myth 16

No One Else Struggles in Marriage Like We Do

The difference between stumbling blocks and stepping stones is how you use them.

–UNKNOWN

L ies, lies, and more lies. No one has a perfect, effortless marriage. Sure, it seems that way—especially if you base your assumptions on social media pictures. But the images are illusions. I know, they look so happy on vacation, and their Christmas card pictures couldn't exude more joy. And the marriage absolutely sounds perfect as she posts about her doting husband who brings her champagne while she takes her nightly bubble bath. She makes sure everyone knows that he is the "best husband ever" #blessed.

But friends, it is not true. No one has the perfect marriage. It is impossible because a marriage is comprised of flawed and fallen human beings. It is foolish to take two broken, imperfect individuals, put them in the same living space, add the responsibility of child-rearing, and expect magical peace and harmony. The truth is, marriage is hard. Relationships are hard. Without putting in effort and sweat equity through the years, it won't work. Period.

Perhaps you feel past the point of no return and are living separate lives. Or perhaps your marriage is over, and the divorce papers are finalized. That is okay. There will be a tomorrow. You will love again. And when you do, the truths I present may help you in the future.

Let me pause to make an important distinction. If you are in an unsafe relationship, get out. Here, I discuss the challenges of making a *safe* marriage work. I am not advocating the preservation of an unsafe one. If your story includes verbal or physical abuse, seek the wisdom and support of local resources and do what you need to protect yourself.

My Story

Instead of presenting a client illustration for this myth, I am going to share my story. I am using my marriage (with Dave's permission) as the example. I could tell you about client couples I have worked with who struggled with feeling alone and disconnected. I could also fill these pages with stories of individual clients who have come to me wondering if they should stick it out or throw in the towel. Instead, I want to tell you my story. I want to share it so you know we *all* struggle. I want you to know that if Dave and I can do it, you can, too.

Our story began on a cold, rainy November night in San Diego in 1997. Dave had just finished his naval aviation flight school training and was sent to begin training in his new plane in San Diego. He had been there for a couple of weeks when a friend of his from flight school invited him to join their group of friends going out for the night.

That same night, I was already dressed down in my comfy clothes, with my hair in a ponytail, ready to call it a night. My roommates, who happened to be friends with Dave's friend, invited me to join them as well. I wasn't feeling up to it. Rainy nights in San Diego are no fun. However, my roommates were relentless, and I finally obliged when they mentioned that the Navy dive bar they were going to was playing '80s music. Done. Sold. Eighties music is my thing, and I get on the dance floor regardless of the fool I make of myself. I changed clothes, freshened up, and went along for the ride, with plans of dancing my "running man" moves like never before.

As soon as we arrived, I noticed Dave with our group of friends. He was so handsome, and he completely caught my eye. While he was sitting down, that is. And then he stood up. Lordy. He is 6' 3" and a whole foot taller than me. We started talking, and with the volume of the music and the mile between our heads, it was difficult to hear him. And, really, let's be honest, I was there to dance. "Pump Up the Jam" was calling. I excused myself and got my groove on.

He turned to my roommate Amanda, and pointing in my direction, he asked, "Now, who is that?" Amanda never misses an opportunity to joke with someone, and thought we would never see him again. "Who, *her*?" she asked, as I was busting a move on the dance floor. "That is Kim. She used to be in a rap band, and her band name is 'Sweaté Kim.'" Does that give you a descriptor of how hard I was dancing? Yep.

For real. Me in a rap band. If you knew me at all, you would know that it is impossible. Sidenote: he believed her. For years. One day after we were married, he asked me about the rap band I was in before I met him. Rap band? What are you talking about? He told me the story. I picked up the phone and immediately called Amanda.

By the sweet grace of God, my fake rap career did not deter him. Somehow he chose to pursue me, regardless of my bad dance moves. Our connection was strong; our love was powerful. A year later, we were married.

Those were the easy years. We were together, young, and having the time of our lives. During that season, no one could tell me there would be difficult seasons to come. I wouldn't have believed them. This amazing man and I would never have troubles—no way. Troubles were for other couples. We loved each other so deeply that we would always work through every disagreement with love and tenderness. Or so I thought.

When I look back on the next twenty years, I marvel at the highs and the lows. I am in awe of the ways we have hurt each other. I can hardly believe we even ended up together with our different wiring and temperaments. How can two people who love each other so much also cause each other such deep pain? But it happens.

Misunderstandings. Dirty diapers. Military deployments. Moves. Financial highs and lows. Technology. Personality differences. Family dynamics. They all take their toll. Before you know it, you look up, and you are struggling to remember each other and make sense of this life you have created together.

Over the years, I have learned so much about marriage—partly through my professional training but mostly through living it out for twenty years. From study and personal experience, I know this is true: no one has the perfect marriage.

Truth 1: Every Marriage Struggles

If you are married, you have felt challenged, frustrated, and disappointed with your spouse. If you haven't, then I am concerned you haven't really opened up your heart to another person. If you haven't been hurt, you haven't been vulnerable. To love is to risk being hurt. In "The Dance," Garth Brooks sings, "I could have missed the pain, but I'd have had to miss the dance." Ah, Garth, how true that intimacy is equal parts bliss and agony.

Actually, dancing is a helpful metaphor for marriage. And, I bet you've had a few missteps. For years, Dave and I stepped on each other's toes. I was trying to cha-cha, and he wanted to samba. He'd move to the cha-cha, but I was off to the foxtrot. Over time, we had to be willing to stay on the

> Marital happiness and lasting unity doesn't just happen; it is a result of effort and labor.

dance floor, and we had to be willing to learn each other's moves. At times, it was too painful for me to dance. And, sometimes, he was not sure which step to take next. The bottom line is this: love is a choice. It is choosing to stay in it until you find your way back into rhythm. It is learning how to fall in sync more quickly.

Hollywood, best-selling romance authors, and magazines sell true love that happens magically, lasts forever, and never loses the fevered pitch of those early days. It can last forever, but not without work and not without embracing change. Marital happiness and lasting unity doesn't just happen; it is a result of effort and labor. Happiness comes when the deep joy of the relationship bubbles over.

Both partners begin marriage with unique expectations about how it is going to be. These expectations are based on family of origin, life experience, temperament, and values. Couples may have dissimilar expectations. Over time, unspoken assumptions lead to conflict. We may feel our spouse is not living up to his end of the commitment just because his version of a good marriage looks different than ours. Presto. Before we know it, we are in the struggle, preparing for battle, and erecting defense walls for protection.

Dr. John Gottman performed years of research in his Seattle "Love Lab" where he monitored couples and tracked their positive and negative relationship skills over a period of time. Gottman uses the metaphor of the Four Horsemen of the Apocalypse to describe the four behaviors that cause couples to struggle:[23]

> **Horseman #1 Criticism**: Criticism means attacking your partner's being, leaving him feeling rejected and assaulted.
>
> **Horseman #2 Contempt:** Contempt—mocking, belittling, despising, and demeaning your spouse— is the single-most reliable predictor of divorce.
>
> **Horseman #3 Defensiveness:** When we feel falsely accused or attacked, defensiveness only makes the disagreement worse.
>
> **Horseman #4 Stonewalling**: When emotionally flooded, we often stonewall, which means shutting down and ignoring our partner with the silent treatment. It can seem like the best option as we seek to protect ourselves from our partner's contempt and criticism.

Gottman's work is particularly impactful because his research in the Love Lab got behind the curtain as he watched real couples in action. He observed couples in their everyday interactions and then distilled the patterns and relationship styles that showed up again and again. When we learn to recognize the horsemen in our marriage, we can work to replace those negative interaction cycles with more positive ones. Choosing carefully how we speak to our spouse is a challenging commitment, but it pays off in stronger

---

23   John Gottman and Nan Silver, *The Seven Principles for Making Marriage Work: A Practical Guide from the Country's Foremost Relationship Expert* (New York: Harmony Books, 1999).

bonds. With a solid foundation, we won't drown, easily lose hope, or give up when the hard times come.

Marriage is not Insta-worthy every moment. Every happy posting reflects years of tenacity and effort. Do you notice the Four Horsemen showing up in your relationship? It will take time and effort to replace destructive patterns with better habits, but noticing is the first step.

Truth 2: We Are All Desperate for Connection

We all need to feel safe and significant. In her book *Hold Me Tight*, Dr. Sue Johnson shares, "Attachment Theory teaches us that our loved one is our shelter in life. When that person is emotionally unavailable or unresponsive, we face being out in the cold, alone and helpless. We are assailed by emotions—anger, sadness, hurt, and, above all, fear . . . Losing connection with our loved one jeopardizes our sense of security . . . We don't think, we feel, we act."[24]

Friends, Dr. Johnson is saying that when we feel like our connection with our loved one is lost, we react before thinking. We have a primal reflex to move into fight or flight. We protest, demand, yell, nag, stonewall, hide, ignore—whatever reaction we naturally default to—to protect ourselves from threat. We come unglued when we don't feel safe or secure in our relationships.

I first learned about this therapy model in 2015 when I went through Emotionally Focused Training (EFT) training in Nashville. Dr. Johnson's model resonated with me. She uses "dance" as a metaphor to explain how couples subconsciously fall into patterns or cycles of relating.

---

24   Sue Johnson, *Hold Me Tight: Seven Conversations for a Lifetime of Love* (New York: Little, Brown and Company, 2008), 30.

As I was sitting in training, watching couples discuss their own relationships, I was shocked to see my relationship with Dave being played out—all the times I've reacted out of fear of lost connection. I thought of him watching TV, which leaves me feeling ignored and shut out, like I don't matter. Because I tell myself he doesn't care, I become angry and nag him about the list of things I need him to complete.

When I nag, he hears me telling him he's failed (which men *love* to hear, by the way), which makes him feel rejected and worthless. So, he shuts me out. He distracts himself and stays busy while stonewalling me, reasoning that if he says nothing, he won't jeopardize the relationship with angry words. He is trying to protect the connection; however, his stonewalling actually makes me feel more anxious, more panicked, and more fearful, which, you guessed it, makes me protest even more loudly. In response, he retreats more. I protest more. He retreats more. Do you see our cycle?

Each relationship has a cycle, though it may include steps and reactions dissimilar to those I describe in my marriage. Friends, here's the truth: the cycle is the problem. Not your spouse. Not you. It's a two-person dance. You make a move, and he responds in kind. Now, infidelity and abuse cannot be blamed on the cycle; there must be accountability there. But, think through the most common struggles you've experienced again and again in your marriage. Consider if, at the core, the fights are really about missed connection and the quest for safety and significance. You both want to know the other is there for you, but that tender message gets buried under the reactions we use to coax the desired reassurance.

The next time you want to nag, give the silent treatment, yell, or demand, stop and ask, "What do I really need?" Is your true desire to feel seen and loved? Ask for that instead. Use soft and inviting words to let your spouse know the true desire of your heart: connection.

Truth 3: We All Need Outside Help

I am grateful to have a husband who is willing to do the work with me. He and I alone can change our marriage and do the hard work of disrupting our negative feedback loops. He and I alone must choose to move toward connection instead of ignoring or yelling. However, we need others to help us see our blind spots. We can't change what we do not see. And, without an impartial third party, it's all too easy for us to rush to blame and resentment.

So, Dave and I have enlisted others to walk with us and cheer us on. To us, the benefit of outside help is clear. Sometimes, we talk to trusted friends or older couples who are further along in their marriage. Often, we use a professional counselor to help us gain fresh insight as we recognize it's hard to practice discernment when you are deep into your own stuff.

Marriage counseling is a resource you should also employ. Objectivity from a qualified individual is priceless. Even counselors struggle in marriage and see other counselors to have a safe space to talk through challenges. No one should feel above asking for help. Marriage is the most precious relationship in your life. God created man and woman for each other, and your children are looking to you to provide a safe, loving home environment. They can sense tension and discord, and unresolved arguments can cause the entire family to feel anxious. Every penny you invest in marriage work is money well spent.

Do This Instead: Work Towards Intimacy

1. Create Space for Your Marriage

Air and sunlight are needed for growth. Don't neglect your marriage by keeping it stuffed into the dark, forgotten recesses of your mind. Bring it out, front and center. Nourish it and give it space.

One way to encourage relational growth is scheduling time together. Make date nights a priority. If money is an issue, find friends to swap kids with and offer each other free childcare. Or put the kids to bed early and cook a romantic dinner together. You can have a date with or without expensive concert tickets and fine dining.

Dave and I have what we call "couch time" (as opposed to TV couch time). During couch time, we sit, sometimes with a glass of wine, and debrief our day. The kids know that during couch time, their job is to leave us alone so we can connect. It is okay to set this boundary with your kids. We go through our Intimacy Statements together, sharing the following:

Intimacy Statements

- Appreciation (something we appreciate that the other did)
- News (something from our day that we haven't shared with the other)
- Puzzles (something we are working through)
- Request for change (something bothering us that we would like to alter)
- Hopes and dreams (something that we hope will happen in the future)

Get creative with ways to create time and space. Sadly, it's quite easy to let other things take priority over your marriage. Don't neglect the urgency of spending time together.

2. Find a Cheerleader/Coach/Counselor

I have a hard time understanding couples who want to do it alone, who see asking for help as weakness. None of us can do it alone. God provides friends and professionals to walk with us, cheer us on, mentor us, coach us, or counsel us. It is such a shame when we pass up the opportunity to be encouraged. You don't get a medal in heaven for toughing out your marriage without help—at least not that I am aware of.

Anything worthwhile in life takes work. For instance, if fitness matters to you, think about the amount of time you invest at the gym. On the low end, maybe it's

> Imagine if you invested in your marriage relationship like you invested in your body.

thirty minutes a day. On the high end, maybe it's more. Imagine if you invested in your marriage relationship like you invested in your body. Or your work. Or your friendships.

Seek out a marriage mentor at your church. Enlist the services of a marriage coach. If you have an EFT therapist or couples therapist in your area, see if he might be a good fit. Attend a marriage weekend away or a retreat. Once you start exploring, you'll find more options than excuses.

3. Create Rituals and Traditions

Rituals and traditions can create a meaningful bond with your spouse and provide another point of connection. Traditions are like beacons, guiding you back to what is essential and most valuable. What location or event would you both enjoy returning to year after year? Maybe it's a special date venue or a resort you love to get away to. Maybe you have a particular way of celebrating each other's birthday.

The details are specific to you, but the principle applies to all. All can experience comfort and connection by making time to do your "thing" as a couple. Gottman describes the positive impact that "rituals" play in the longevity of

> Intentionality is a powerful component of a positive relationship.

relationships. He encourages couples to begin and end each day with rituals.[25] Rituals can look like this:

Rituals

- Stress-reducing conversations
- Shared meals (no screens)
- Good morning kisses
- Welcome home hugs
- Family meetings
- Date nights
- Vacations
- Lunch out after church

Intentionality is a powerful component of a positive relationship. Life gets in the way, and before we know it, we are standing on opposite sides of the dance floor. We must pursue each other. We must put the marriage first.

---

25 John Gottman and Nan Silver, *The Seven Principles for Making Marriage Work* (New York: Three Rivers Press, Crown Publishing Group imprint, 1999).

What can you do today to get unstuck in your marriage? Have you been giving each other the cold shoulder for a month? Are you not on the same page with a big decision? Have you given up on connection because this season of raising kids feels too busy? Take time to identify the patterns of relating that are keeping you at odds with each other. It's not too late to learn a new way to groove together.

Reflection Questions (If Currently in a Relationship):

1. Are you intentional about connection in your relationship? Does your spouse share your desire to prioritize connection?
2. How can you be intentional about investing in your relationship together?
3. Do deeper feelings of shame, vulnerability, or fear get in the way of connection? Which issues need to be addressed now?

Reflection Questions (If Currently Not in a Relationship):

1. Do you notice a missing element of connection in past relationships?
2. How can you use this time of singleness to work on yourself and the ways you engage with others?
3. Do deeper feelings of shame, vulnerability, or fear get in the way of connecting with others? Which issues need to be addressed now?

New Insight:

_____

_____
_____
_____
_____
_____
_____
_____
_____
_____
_____
_____
_____
_____
_____
_____
_____
_____
_____
_____
_____
_____

Conclusion

Obstacles and setbacks are part of life. It is our job to make sure they don't keep us stuck, block us from emotional intimacy with others, or lead us to mistreat ourselves. We will never realize our full potential or live out our calling while weighed down by thoughts of defeat. Stop believing the myths that you tell yourself to settle, stay small, and play it safe.

Friends, we are all created for greatness. You are valuable. You are enough. I encourage you today to think about where you are on your journey. Where might you be stuck? If you identified with any of these myths, today is the day to make a change. You must let them go. Put this book down and take a moment to reflect. Work through the questions in the back of the book. Reflect in your own journal. Put a stake in the ground. Make this the day you step into wholeness. Create your action steps. How can you move toward your best life?

Speaking from experience, I'll admit it's not as easy as just letting go of lies and being done with faulty beliefs. Our thinking patterns have been with us a long time, maybe all our lives. It takes practice to capture defeating thoughts and filter them through God's truth, but you have to begin somewhere, sometime. Begin today. You are worth it, and until you face these lies head-on, you won't reach your full potential.

Much is at stake. We not only have the rest of our lives to consider, but we also must consider our legacy. When we act against whatever is holding us back, we can then teach our *kids* how to reach *their* fullest potential. We can't teach what we don't know. They are watching our example. What message are you sending? That life is amazing and their potential is limitless? Or that life is hard and must be endured?

Today is the day you get to let go of old habits and patterns. Today is the day you begin again. When you identify and then move past obstacles, you'll be able to give the world the gift you were meant to give.

This is a shout-out to all women. Every single one of us. If we all decide this is the day to lay down these obstacles and quit believing these myths, can you imagine the impact we could have on the world? We need to rally, support each other, and hold each other accountable.

Can you even imagine what would happen with everyone in full pursuit of the life each is meant to live and the legacy each is meant to leave? We could change the world, right now. The impact could be astonishing. This is your time, my friend. No more hiding. No more excuses. No more waiting for the perfect circumstances or timing. You were made by the Creator of the universe to rise. We need your impact on this world.

You are created to shine. You are created to soar. You are amazing. Now start living like it!

About the Author

Kim Anderson is a board-certified licensed therapist, certified life coach, speaker, and team builder. She is also co-host of the iTunes Podcast *Coming Unglued*, which provides skills and tools for women to become unstuck and live free. Kim works with clients, helping them overcome limiting beliefs that keep them glued to grief, or worse, anxious, depressed, and hopeless. She also leads  retreats and corporate team-building events that help individuals and teams identify the best ways to break free of disconnection and work together towards a common goal of connection, listening, and learning in the workplace. Kim has one mission in mind in both her personal and professional life: to lead with love and let go of limitations.

Appendix

Deeper Application

O ther chapters of your life are waiting to be written; bold plot twists and happy endings are still possible. Stop dreaming and start doing. You are created for more, and we need *you*. Let's get unstuck together!

You can download your own blank templates at

www.kimanderson.life/free-download

Mindfulness Exercise (Myth 2)

You can learn to practice mindfulness in many wonderful ways. Mindfulness, in essence, is noticing your thoughts, feelings, and bodily sensations and using that awareness to ground yourself in the present. You can search online to find other helpful resources, but here is one of my favorite exercises:

Mindfulness Exercise

When you feel distressed, take a moment to yourself. If you are able, lie flat on your back with your eyes closed, taking in deep breaths, inhaling and exhaling. Observe your thoughts for ten minutes. Don't try to clear your head, simply notice what is coming up for you. Examine your thoughts without judgement or labeling. Just be present with them. Pay attention to any tension in your body and focus on relaxing your muscles. Give yourself permission to just be still. Afterwards, reflect on any new awareness that came out of this exercise.

Clarifying Values (Myth 3)

Rate each value on a scale of one to ten, with one being the lowest value and ten being the highest value. Go back and circle the five highest numbers to identify the values that are most important to you. Keep these values in mind as you are determining your purpose.

Value

____Accomplishment	____Justice
____Adventure	____Leadership
____Beauty	____Loyalty
____Catalyst	____Mastery
____Commitment	____Pleasure
____Compassion	____Relatedness
____Consistency	____Responsibility
____Contributions / Service	____Security
____Creativity	____Sensitivity / Niceness
____Discovery / Learning	____Spirituality / God
____Emotions / Feelings	____Teaching
____Family	____Winning
____Freedom	

Purpose Questionnaire (Myth 3)

Purpose Questionnaire

What motivates you?

_____

What makes you feel good about yourself?

_____

What are you doing when you feel your best?

_____

Why do you live where you do?

_____

Why do you travel where you do?

_____

What is important to you in relationship?

_____

What do you read and watch on TV? And why?

_____

What do you love?

_____

What do you hate?

_____

What would you do if you had all the resources in the world and knew you coudn't fail?

_____

What gives you energy?

_____

What drains your energy?

_____

Who do you want to help?

_____

How can you help?

_____

Blank ABCD Chart (Myth 4)

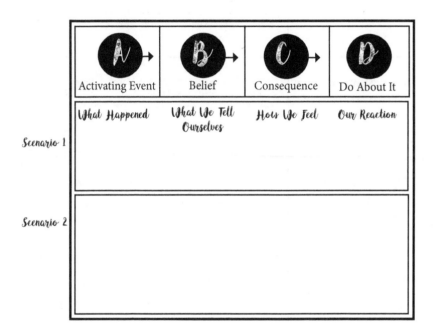

Setting Boundaries (Myth 6)

It is okay to simply say no to something that doesn't work for you. It is not necessary to explain why. If you feel the need to explain, do so in a way that protects you and doesn't leave your no open to negotiation. Remember, if you don't engage in self-care, you won't have anything left over to give to those you love.

I love the sandwich method. Think of your no as a sandwich with bread on both sides and meat in the middle. The meat is your no and the bread is softening it with kindness. See examples below. Remember, the person who doesn't respect your boundary is the one with the problem.

Boundary Violation	Boundaried Response
Family members are visiting too often.	We love seeing you and are grateful for your effort (bread), but we have learned that we need some time together as a family as well (meat). Perhaps we could schedule some time for you to visit a few months out (bread)?
Friends are expecting you to participate in every gathering.	You are all so special to me (bread). I love hanging out with you, but I am wired to need more time to recharge (meat). I'll haev to catch up with you at the next event (bread).
The school PTO wants you to be president.	I am honored you think I would be good in this role (bread). Unfortunately, I'm not able to take on any additional roles due to my schedule (meat). I would love to offer support as needed (bread).
Your son's soccer team wants you to be the team parent.	I am honored you think I would be good in this role (bread). Unfortunately, I'm not able to take on any additional roles due to my schedule (meat). I would love to offer support as needed (bread). What other needs do you have?

Life Balance Wheel (Myth 8)

To ensure healthy balance in life, it is necessary to stop periodically and assess where we need to invest energy. Balance is relative to each individual, so my life balance wheel won't look like your wheel. Nor should it.

Below is an example life balance wheel I often use in coaching. It gives us a "helicopter view" of life, helping us identify what is going well and what needs extra attention. Take a moment to reflect on each category and then rate it based on the amount of attention you are currently giving that specific area. When you are done, connect the spokes so you can see where you are fulfilled and where you might want to invest energy.

After you have identified the gap between where you are now and where you want to be, take action. Create a plan, work with a coach, or find an accountability partner to help you move toward the life you desire.

Sample Completed Wheel:

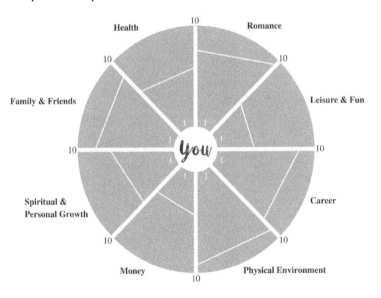

Blank Wheel:

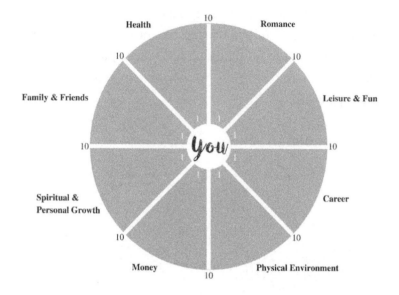

SMART Goals Chart (Myth 10)

Sample Chart:

Specific	I want to be an elementary teacher in my district, in two years.
Measureable	I will be hired by my school district.
Attainable	I have all the resources I need to become a teacher.
Realistic	I have all the skills I need to become a teacher.
Timely	I have a schedule and a plan.

Blank Chart:

Specific	
Measureable	
Attainable	
Realistic	
Timely	

If/Then Chart (Myth 12)

Write your fear or worry under the top left "what if," followed by "then" to the right. Move the "then" to the next row under "what if," and then answer the "then." Keep working this through, until you reach a dead end. I believe that you are capable of handling the scenario at the end. Remember, it is just fear telling you otherwise.

Sample Chart:

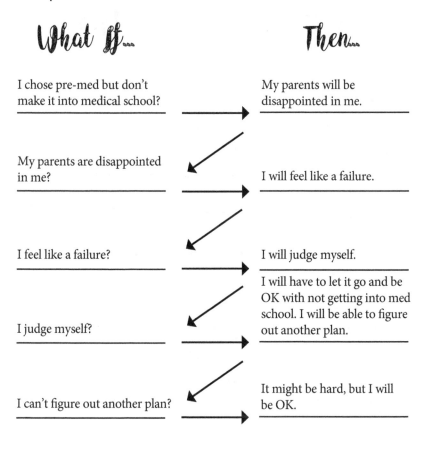

What If...

Then...

What If...	Then...
I chose pre-med but don't make it into medical school?	My parents will be disappointed in me.
My parents are disappointed in me?	I will feel like a failure.
I feel like a failure?	I will judge myself.
I judge myself?	I will have to let it go and be OK with not getting into med school. I will be able to figure out another plan.
I can't figure out another plan?	It might be hard, but I will be OK.

Blank Chart:

What If...   Then...

_____ ⟶ _____

_____ ⟶ _____

_____ ⟶ _____

_____ ⟶ _____

_____ ⟶ _____

Blank Chart:

What If...   Then...

_____   ——▶   _____

_____   ——▶   _____

_____   ——▶   _____

_____   ——▶   _____

_____   ——▶   _____

Printed in the USA
CPSIA information can be obtained
at www.ICGtesting.com
JSHW022332140824
68134JS00019B/1443